SINGLES CARE
ONE FOR ANOTHER

Karen Greenwaldt

D1190829

DISCIPLESHIP RESOURCES

MATERIALS FOR GROWTH IN CHRISTIAN FAITH AND LIFE

P.O. Box 189 • Nashville, TN 37202 • Phone (615) 340-7284

Revised 1991.

ISBN 0-88177-072-8

Library of Congress Catalog Card No. 89-50374

DR072B

CONTENTS

TO THE CAREGIVERS

You are, have been, or will be "single" at some point in your life. As you know, single adults make up a vast portion of our population. Many are single by choice. Others are single by circumstance. Some are divorced, others are widowed, and still others have always been single. Some are parents, and many others are aunts, uncles, sons, daughters, and friends.

Almost one-half of our population is single. The Census Bureau says that four in every ten adults are single. By the year 2000, the Bureau projects that one of every two adults will be single. That is a sizeable population! Millions upon millions of persons need our concern and care.

Communities have recognized that single adults are an attractive customer cluster. Restaurants, night spots, and specialized stores are built for them. Advertising accounts of consumer products often recognize their buying potential by packaging meals for singles, by planning Club Med vacations, and by expanding condominium and apartment complexes.

Yet, consistently, single adults are missing in large numbers from our churches. Program planners, pastors, and key leaders frequently do not consider single adults as an audience for ministry.

The focus on ministry with traditional families has often discouraged planning for single adults. Yet, single adults make up a vast network of families and friends. Often creating their own supporting and nurturing units, these single adults form biological and chosen family units. But these family units are often not recognized by the congregation, which frequently insists on ministry to couples with their 1.6 children.

Similar to other neglected groups, single adults form strong, caring bonds one with another. These bonds often create communities of people who listen, support, challenge, and care for each other.

Many elements bind these persons together in communities of faith. Some single adults form relationships with single parents—others with single career associates, others with divorced persons, and still others with persons who have lost someone to death. And still others form strong relationships with married friends. Perhaps the strongest bonding element is found in the word *single*. Its rallying force can be seen in communities of all sizes. Whether named formally or not, many single people look for others like themselves, others who are single or for those who love and support them as singles.

"I go to movies and to dinner with my friends. We don't have dates on Fridays, so we go out together."

"I go to the grocery store and notice who is single. You can tell by what's in the shopping cart. If I'm interested in someone I see, I introduce myself."

"I joined a singles club because they offer activities for me and my friends. We have fun together and talk about things that matter too."

"I searched for other single parents in my town. We formed a baby-sitting co-op first. Then we became great friends who then invited married women to join us."

Single—a reality for many people. *Single*—a rallying word to organize and care for others. Single—an audience in our population which deserves the attention of the church—if the church intends to accept all of God's children.

Many individuals and congregations respond to the word *single*. Tremendously effective programs and caring acts are evident. But many more individuals and churches need to respond. This book is intended to inspire those who are in ministry with single adults and those who want to be.

As individuals and as people together, we have many opportunities to "be the church" to other persons in our towns or communities. The church means many things. Here are some definitions:

- Sharing love and friendship with others
- Caring in specific and concrete ways
- Accepting others
- Telling others about the love of God at all times and in all places
- Being there when persons experience trauma or joy
- Supporting and listening
- Referring persons to appropriate helping agencies and groups
- Working to overcome injustices within community systems

The writer of 1 John 4:19 says, "We love because [God] first loved us." Because of that love made known to us through Jesus Christ, we are called to respond—because we must respond to the gracious gifts of God.

Throughout the scriptures, examples of God's care are found, and people respond. So it is with single adults. As adults in society, we who are both single and married, have experienced pain and joy, suffering and peace. There are days when we feel all alone, and there are other days when we cannot escape the crowds. In these experiences, caring is extended to us. At times we accept that care and at other times we reject it. At times, we acknowledge this care as a gift from God. On the other hand, there are moments when we are sure that the caring act is a direct affront, which has nothing to do with God's love.

So it is with other single adults in our communities. They, too, experience God's caring through others as both gift and curse. Yet, as Christian persons, there are wonderful opportunities to be the church to others. The challenge is to learn and practice caring in appropriate ways.

As one part of the Body of Christ in the world, we daily have chances to respond to others in our communities. In the parable of the Samaritan, Jesus tells the story of the man who chose not to pass by the one who had been beaten, robbed, and left in the ditch. Just as the Samaritan, the Priest, and the Levite made choices related to the man in the ditch, so we also have opportunities to respond.

This manual intends to help each reader consider choices for caregiving with single adults. The beginning chapters suggest various types of single adults by presenting stories and images of persons living in our communities. Following each description are suggestions for ways to respond to individuals and groups of single adults.

The next part of the manual contains material for the person who wants to form groups of single adults who care for each other and for individuals in the community. Suggestions for beginning and expanding programs, worksheets, and ideas for leaders are included.

The final section of the manual contains resource lists and other information for both individual single adults and for leaders in single adult programs.

As you read these pages, begin by reading about the type of single adult with whom you feel the most empathy. You may be a member of that group, or you may have a close friend or relative who is like that type of single adult. As you read the suggestions for ways to care for that person, consider how you are already giving care. Then consider what else you might do.

As you read, remember that the most caring act is one which expresses yourself to another person. Therefore, your choices—either as an individual or as a group of single adults—should be genuine rather than contrived.

It costs you something to care for another person, and you may find yourself entering into a world of pain and joy. You, at times, may feel hurt by the responses of others. Caring for others is not always safe, but it most usually is rewarding. For as you care for others, so your sense of caring for yourself increases.

Remember, "We love because God first loved us." God, who through a single person, Jesus, made love known to us and who created all individuals for community, calls each of us to be in ministry. The challenge is before us. We can care one for another, and be assured that God goes with us as we care for others.

PART ONE
Caring for Single Adults

A story and study guide for individuals and groups who "have been called, with all humility and gentleness, with patience, bearing with one another in love, making every effort to maintain the unity of the Spirit in the bond of peace" (Ephesians 4:1-3).

1. SINGLE ADULTS IN CRISIS

Ray and Julie lived together for six years. They always meant to get married, but excuses kept creeping into their discussions. At first, the excuses seemingly were trivial, "If you'd lose 13 pounds, I'd marry you," Or "If you'd quit smoking, I'd marry you." Neither would do the things that the other wanted, so they kept postponing the wedding date.

With each change in plans, both Ray and Julie said, "It's easier to live together rather than go through the hassle of getting married. Our parents wish we'd do the legal thing, but we don't want to do that until . . . "

As the years progressed, Ray and Julie became more and more entwined in each other's lives. For all outward appearances, they were presumed to be married by most of their friends. They never bothered to tell the truth about their relationship.

At a party, Ray met a delightful woman who was intriguing to him. Fascinated by her eyes and the way she moved among the guests, Ray decided to introduce himself to her. What followed could be best described by Ray. "I never met a woman like her. Here I am committed to Julie, and yet I can't keep my eyes off Elizabeth. She's like the gentle wind that blows away the mist in the early morning. Her voice is like a symphony of chimes. I don't know what I'm going to do, except that I will see her again. She's like magic and I'm drawn irresistibly to her. What will I tell Julie?"

Later Julie asked Ray where he had been during the party, and he lied, saying, "Oh, I went for a walk to get away from the crowd for a while." Julie wondered about his answer because she had seen him talking to a "gorgeous woman who seemed like she would steal him away in a minute." Julie did not tell Ray about her feelings, believing that she had just not seen correctly what had happened.

Ray began to stay out later in the evenings and received strange phone calls from persons who hung up if Julie answered the phone. Julie felt more and more uneasy, but she "loved Ray and I believed his answers to my questions."

Then one day, Julie saw Ray and Elizabeth together. "I knew the answers to my questions without asking them again. I knew where Ray had been spending his evenings, and I knew our relationship was over.

How could he do that to me? I gave him my life and he threw it back to me."

Days went by while Julie decided what to do. "I didn't tell Ray what was wrong even though he kept asking. I just didn't care any more. It didn't seem worth the energy to yell or cry or do anything at all." Julie stayed home one day. "I told the office I was sick. I really guess I was. I packed up everything that was mine or that I wanted from what we had bought together. I left. I didn't leave a note for Ray. And that felt good. Let him wonder for a while. I miss him, feel empty without him, but I don't think I can ever trust him again. He called me at work one day, but I refused to talk to him. He hasn't called since. So it's over and I'll pick up the pieces of my life."

Jocelyn is anorexic. Early in her treatment program, she said, "I feel like everyone looks at me and says, 'Look at how fat she is.' I really hate myself because I can't seem to lose any more weight. But I'll keep trying. Someday I'll fit into that size 5 pair of slacks."

Jocelyn is 5'8" and weighs less than 110 pounds. That was not always the case. While in college and during her marriage, Jocelyn weighed an attractive 137 pounds. She was the campus beauty and considered modeling for a career. Yet, something about modeling didn't fit her value system. "I couldn't buy the idea that I might use my body to sell things. I looked great in the pictures. The clothes were stunning, and I enjoyed the glamorous life. . . . But one day, I met a young woman who said she wanted to look like me. She never would! She was not unattractive, but she would never be like me. I thought about her for several days. I decided that I didn't want to be someone whom others wanted to be like. I wanted people to like being who they are and I just didn't think that I wanted to support the clothing industry by selling myself. I'm more important than that.

"Before I quit modeling for the department store, I was talking to my boss about my decision. She said to me, 'Jocelyn, you'd never make it anyway. You're too fat for a big-time modeling career.' I guess her words tapped into some strange fear that I'd been carrying around in me for a long time. I was afraid that I was fat. In fact, I'd always worried about it. I've always started a new diet each week. Well, I guess I went a bit crazy.

"I didn't want to be a model, but I didn't want to be fat either. So, I quit eating. I only ate saltine crackers for six months. My husband couldn't understand what was wrong with me. My problems became the excuse for his desire to leave. He said he didn't like being around me any more. He left, and that's when I got sick. At the hospital, I found out what was wrong: I am anorexic. I'm in treatment now, but I'll always have to live with the suspicion that 'I'm fat.'"

Clay is dying. He doesn't want to tell anyone. "I'm not sick enough yet, and people just think I'm working too hard. Someday, they will know what's wrong, but I'm not ready to tell them."

While living in a rundown apartment, Clay has existed in the fringes of the working world for years. His best friends are addicts, and "even though I've never been one, I'm around them a lot." One night several years ago, Clay was invited to a party with his friends. "I knew they'd be using, but I thought I could just go along for the fun of it. Besides, no one ever got caught, and no one really was that bad off. I went to the party, and it was the worst night of my life. There were some strange people there, and toward the end of the party, they all ganged up on me. Before I knew what was happening, I was being forced to shoot up. I never had done that before, and I didn't really want to. Somehow it was important for me to be accepted by this new group of people."

The needle was dirty, and Clay is now living with the knowledge that he will die. "The name of my death is AIDS. I did it to myself. I don't know why, but it's the ultimate consequence of a stupid act."

His family has deserted him, and most of his friends have disappeared. Some of them have died, others have moved on, and others are afraid "that they will catch it from me. I used to go to church. Now I'm afraid to go. Some of the members know what's wrong with me. They told me to stay away. I can't convince them that they can't catch this thing from me. I'm not dangerous to their children, and I'm not using drugs. They think I am. I told them my story, and now they use it against me. Oh well, I guess I'll just spend my last days with the few people who still think I'm an okay guy."

CAREGIVING WITH SINGLE ADULTS WHO ARE IN CRISIS

The types of crises are as varied as the single adults themselves. When looking in on the lives of these adults, we are tempted at times to trivialize the crisis moments. For single adults, crisis can range from lack of commitment or illness to such moments as the death of a pet, the loss of a job, the moving of a friend, the death of a parent, the loss of a friend, stress at work or school, and so on.

As with caregiving with all single adults, caring for these persons must be done appropriately and with respect.

For some single adults, caring is found in the referrals you suggest. For others, caring is most appropriate when you act in specific ways. Talk to the single adult, listen for suggestions of ways to care, and follow through with significant actions.

As an Individual, You Might:

1. Learn about the crisis from the single adult or from others who know that person.

2. Visit with your friend in order to assess what the crisis is. By listening, you can determine various actions which might be appropriate.

3. Never laugh at the feelings another person is experiencing. The crisis your friend is having may seem trivial to you. Yet, for your friend, the feelings are real and must be attended to carefully.

4. Take time to listen. Make telephone calls when you have time to talk. Visit with the person when your schedule is not crowded.

5. Learn about the resources available in your community. For example, know how to locate organizations such as Alcoholics Anonymous, Narcotics Anonymous, Sexual Addiction Anonymous, etc. Know how to find agencies or churches which provide for emergency food and shelter. Be aware of local clinics which offer medical, legal, and financial services on sliding fee scales.

6. Refer when you feel overwhelmed or if you feel threatened (physically, emotionally, theologically, etc.). Referral is not a sign of weakness on your part. Caring means knowing when you can help and when you can't.

7. Assess the amount of danger confronting the other person. If you need to call the police, do so. If you need to call in other persons to help (your pastor, a nextdoor neighbor, a member of an anonymous group, etc.), do so.

8. If you feel uncomfortable with persons who need to cry, feel anger, or express other emotions, find ways to deal with your own feelings. Learn why you react the way you do. Know when you need to take care of yourself and when you can be useful to another person.

9. Give advice and answers sparingly. At times, single adults who are in crisis need advice. Usually, persons carry in themselves the knowledge of how best to care for themselves. Help them sort out their options for dealing with the crisis, and support them in their decisions.

10. Know the stages of grief and loss. Help these single adults recognize that their reaction to the crisis may have elements of mourning for

that which has been lost. Talk with your friends about how their reactions are normal.

11. If your friend begins to talk about God's will and part in the crisis, help him or her to sort out what is God's will and what is not. (See the resource list for suggestions on this topic.)

12. Introduce your friend to others who have gone through similar types of crises. Help your friend to find the support that comes from talking with another person who has gone through a crisis and survived it.

13. Suggest groups, classes, etc., which might provide the information your friend needs to overcome the crisis.

14. Invite your friend to go with you to worship or other activities at the church. Suggest other things your friend might do with you "to get his/her mind off the crisis." Sometimes distance is needed from the crisis in order to come back to it later with fresh ideas on how to cope. Therefore, help your friend find ways to relax and play.

15. Suggest a book to read, a movie to see, etc., that might help your friend see new options for dealing with the crisis.

16. Support the children and other family members of those who are in crisis. Refer these persons to social service or church groups who can provide support. Refer to the suggestions for caring for single parent families.

● *Add your own ideas, here:*

As a Group, You Might:

1. Discuss techniques for intervention to be used when you know that a person is experiencing a crisis.

2. Provide ways for persons to interact on levels which are more than social. When persons are in crisis, they need to know who in a group can be trusted or who will provide support.

3. Talk about coping strategies for various crises. Help persons foresee ways they can care for themselves in the eventuality of a crisis.

4. Provide a resource list of agencies, groups, etc., which provide crisis services. Make that list available in places where it can be obtained anonymously. These lists might include mental health groups, counselors, physicians, etc., for those in emotional crises. Or they might include names of persons who can provide legal aid, financial support, or other special services through agencies. In addition, they can include suggestions for finding support systems for the children and other family members of persons who are in crisis.

5. Learn the signs of addiction, abuse, emotional trouble, etc. Be ready to offer support and intervention when needed. If you plan an intervention, be sure to talk with counselors about appropriate methods and follow-up strategies.

6. Be aware of plant closings, farm auctions, and other signs of economic distress. Pay attention to the needs of single adults who may be caught in crisis.

7. Plan a study session on the role of God in crisis. Help persons develop their own theology or belief system for considering God's action in the midst of crisis. (See the resource pages for suggestions.)

8. Pray for those in crisis, both those you know personally and those whom you do not know.

9. Support financially and through volunteer labor those community agencies and groups which provide services for those in crisis.

10. Talk about standards of behavior expected for persons who participate in group activities. Intervene when those standards are broken.

11. Offer grief recovery workshops, seminars, or support groups for persons who are dealing with the loss of someone they have dated (or lived with) for years.

12. Provide settings in which persons can discuss the health of their relationships. Suggest ideas for dealing with relationships which may be harmful to persons. Be supportive of persons who choose relationships which may not be ideal. Help those persons consider the consequences

which may result. Offer support to these persons regardless of their decisions.

13. Participate in training so that you will know the most effective ways to care for those who are in crisis. What a person in crisis does not need is a "do gooder," a person who cares but who doesn't have the skills needed to care constructively.

● *Add your own ideas here:*

Remember that caregiving with persons who are in the midst of crisis or who are recovering from a crisis must be planned carefully. Each crisis is different and each response is different. Pay attention to the cries for help that may be made. Be willing to intervene if that action is appropriate. Refer when necessary, but find ways to support the single adults even if you refer them to other sources of help.

Caring for those in crisis takes commitment. That care is not given quickly. Often, caregiving may extend for several weeks, months, and maybe years. Consider your own expectations for caring. If you cannot or will not commit to care for some persons for a long period of time, find someone who can.

Be aware that you may or may not be the right person to help in the midst of a crisis. Consider your skills as a caregiver for those in crisis, and respond appropriately.

2. SINGLE PARENTS

Carl's divorce was final a few weeks ago. That fact didn't make the news in his town. But all of his friends were talking about the fact that Carl was awarded custody of his sixteen-month-old son. That just doesn't happen in Carl's town!

"What will you do to take care of Peter?" asked Carl's mother. "You have to get to work at 7:15 every day, and on weekends you'll have to do all the shopping, washing, paying bills. . . . What will you do?"

"I'm not sure what I'll do long term, but I've found a friend who'll keep Peter during the day for me. She's a member of our church, and she loves children. MaryBeth will get to our house early enough to fix breakfast for all of us. Then, I'll feed Peter, and run out the door at 7:00. MaryBeth will stay with him all day. She'll be like his grandmother, I hope. She'll fix supper, and when I get home, she'll leave. That may not work forever, but MaryBeth is willing to try it, and so am I."

Days went by, and the arrangement with MaryBeth worked well. What didn't work well was Carl's relationship with some of his friends. "They act like I have the plague. I guess they think I can't be a good father to Peter. What do I know about raising an infant? I never learned about that anywhere. I never thought I'd have to know how to take care of all those problems. I thought I'd share those responsibilities. And I suppose I really thought Sally would do most of the child care until Peter was older. My friends must think I'm crazy. Sometimes, I think I am too. Some of them really ignore me. That hurts. I never thought I'd lose my friends as well as my wife."

The persons at Carl's office are very supportive, giving him time off to arrange for Peter's care and to take care of other issues. "I need to find someone to talk to about what's going on in my head. I feel like part of me has been cut off. I know in my head that those feelings must be normal, but sometimes, I just can't stop crying. I didn't want this divorce. I thought we could work out our differences. But how can I live with knowing that she preferred another man to me? That just sends me off. Either I cry or I want to kill her, sometimes him, and then I just feel nothing—like I don't exist."

"I know I'll survive all of this. At least that's what my pastor says. Without him and some of my friends at church, I'd really lose it. Sometimes I don't believe I'll make it, but with them telling me that I will, I keep trying."

Rebecca's husband died fourteen years ago. "I remember the day so well. Our son's birthday was that day, and our daughter finished first place in a debate competition. And then I got the call that Frank had had a heart attack at work. . . .

"Fourteen years of living alone with two children. Now they're grown, but I always wonder what life for them and me would have been like if Frank had lived longer. I've done the best I could with raising them. Sometimes, I didn't think I could take on one more crisis. Those teenage years were pretty bad, especially when Tom had his car wreck and Jennifer broke her jaw.

"But I made it. I remember thinking that if I could just escape to the bathroom for some quiet time, I'd be okay. They used to bang on the door, and tell me to come out 'to see' something. I'd get so mad. One day I told them never to bother me when I was in the bathroom. That was the day the curtains in the kitchen caught on fire. They didn't tell me. I smelled the smoke—I gave them thunder about that. All they said was, 'Well, you told us not to bother you.' That was the day when I called my parents and cried for twenty minutes. They just listened to me and said, 'Now, now,' and I felt better. They didn't give advice very often, but when they did, I listened. I didn't always appreciate their words, but I knew they cared."

Fourteen years as a single parent have been hard ones for Rebecca. She says that what helped her through those years were caring and supportive friends and parents. "I read all kinds of books and articles, but the most help was to talk about what it was like, especially during those teenage years."

CAREGIVING WITH SINGLE PARENTS

All single parents are different. Their stories often amuse us and them. Sometimes their stories make us cry with tears of pain and understanding. Each act of caring for single parents is different because the needs of parents are never the same. As we care for single parents, we must always listen to their stories in order to assess what types of caring would be most useful and appreciated.

In addition, when we care for single parents, we must be certain that we care in appropriate ways. First, we ask a person's permission to care.

Sometimes, we do that directly. At other times, we can ask permission by observing and responding in appropriate ways. Then we can talk about whether that act of caring was helpful.

Remember that the single parent is most likely already juggling a full schedule. You will not want to add to the burden of that schedule. As you choose to care for a single parent, you may want to talk with persons who have lived as single parents for a longer period of time. You can learn much from them as you seek to know what "the most caring act could be."

You may be a single parent yourself. When caring for others, pay attention to the acts of caring that have meant the most to you. Consider if similar gifts of care would be appropriate for another person.

If you are not a single parent, find someone to talk with. Try to understand what it feels like to be single and a parent. Listen for examples of ways you might care.

In addition, look at the following lists of ideas for caring. One list suggests what individuals can do to care. The other list proposes what people can offer to single parents individually or in groups.

As an Individual, You Might:
1. Send a card or note expressing warm wishes.
2. Take a fully cooked meal on an evening when the single parent has experienced a "terrible" day.
3. Send a check for any amount of money.
4. Stay with the children while the parent goes shopping or takes a nap.
5. Offer to keep the children for a weekend or other time.
6. Water plants, collect the mail, etc., when the parent and the children go on vacation.
7. *Really* listen to the feelings and thoughts of the parent.
8. Sit with the family in church and help with the younger children.
9. Take a sack of groceries to the family when there is illness.
10. Loan your car or help when the parent's car needs repair.
11. Offer to provide transportation for the children.
12. Be an advocate for child care and child support payment laws, etc., with community, state, and nationally elected persons.
13. Be aware of the life changes of the children and their impact on the single parents, and respond appropriately (i.e., changes in school, graduations, dating relationships, engagements, marriages, birth of children, moving back home after college, etc.).

14. Provide respite care for single parents with children who are disabled physically, emotionally, or mentally.

15. Help single parents find appropriate opposite-sex role models for their children, or offer your own friendship and support to the children.

16. Send birthday cards (and other greetings) to single parents and to their children.

● *Add your own ideas here:*

As a Group, You Might:

1. Offer a support group for parents (one for custodial parents and one for non-custodial parents).

2. Offer a support group for children of various ages.

3. Provide connections between parents of children of various ages (i.e., link parents of young children together, parents of college-age children together, etc.).

4. Provide child care services for the parent during all single adult group functions.

5. Plan a short-term educational program designed to help single parents "be the best parent" they can be.

6. Provide a toy and clothing exchange program for single parent families.

7. Link families together for holiday celebrations.

8. Plan ways to connect single adults with single parent families for mutual support and affirmation.

9. Offer some activities to which children of single parent families are invited.

10. Create child care clubs in which persons share time as sitters.

11. Give a donation to a family which has financial trouble.

12. Provide a coupon exchange program or a magazine exchange program.

13. Develop a health check-up program for single parents and their children. Recruit doctors and nurses to provide medical services at low cost to participants.

14. Provide brochures which list qualified, low-cost legal, financial, and counseling services.

15. Offer classes or groups to help persons deal with grief issues (i.e., issues of loss felt when children go to kindergarten, grade school, middle/ junior high, high school, college, technical school, military services, new apartments, etc.).

16. Provide support groups or literature for single parents when their children become engaged, marry, divorce, have children, or experience other life changes.

● *Add your own ideas here:*

As you care for single parents, remember that their time and yours is valuable. Therefore, plan ways to care which are appropriate to the relationship that you have with the single parent. As you care one for another, risk caring in ways that are specific and immediate. Plan your caring so that your actions are seen as genuine rather than as paternalistic. If you are not sure how to care for single parents, ask the parents and the children. Listen carefully for the feelings and undertones of emotion. By paying attention, you can learn new ways to care genuinely and appropriately.

3. SINGLE ADULTS WHO ARE BEREAVED

Rachel went to a funeral five months ago. When she talks about it, she cries. Usually, she does not talk about it. She cannot admit yet that the funeral was for her husband, Jonathan. When she admits that she went to a funeral, she says, "It was lovely—You know, I was really close to that person."

Rachel's friends do not know what to do with her denial of Jonathan's death. They tell her, cruelly it seems to them, that he has died and that she went to his funeral. They tell Rachel about the flowers, the music, the people who were there, and Rachel looks at them blankly as if they are speaking in another language.

The phrase "What can we do for her?" echoes throughout their conversations. No one has any ideas left. Some still believe that Rachel needs professional help, but getting her to talk with a counselor seems like a distant possibility.

Most of the time Rachel functions as if nothing significant has happened in her life. She goes to work, feeds the cat, goes shopping, cooks her meals, and attends worship. For most people who interact with her, Rachel seems quite normal. "It's hard to believe that Jonathan died," they say. "She seems so normal and natural. She really is handling these changes in her life so well."

But her friends know differently. Rachel is not handling her life well. There seems to be a door that is closed inside her. Her eyes look vacant much of the time, except when she visits with her niece's children. At those times, Rachel really does seem all right. She laughs, plays, tells stories, and enjoys herself immensely.

It's when she goes home to the routine of her life that the door closes again, and Rachel seems to disappear behind the mask of "I'm fine."

Michael works very hard as a taxi driver. Hours that he works are long, and his fares are usually harried business people who rarely say hello to him. For them, Michael is part of the machinery that moves them from one place to another. Occasionally, a fare gets in his cab and starts to talk to him. At those times, Michael wishes he could drop through a hole in the floor of his cab and disappear.

"How's your day been?" they ask, or, "What's new with you?" Michael

15

despises those questions. Those questions are "so hard! They can't know what is going through my mind!! How would they like it if I told them that in the last six months, I've lost my wife, my mother, and a cousin? My wife divorced me. My mother and my cousin both died of cancer—I'm not sure which is worse. I expected my wife to leave, but I didn't expect my mother and cousin to die."

Michael's feelings are all mixed up. "I feel like I've been stomped on and ground up into little pieces. My life has completely changed, and some fare gets in and asks, 'How are ya?' How am I? I don't know, but I'd like to kick the next fare that asks me anything other than how to get to some office or restaurant!"

Michael has a few friends that are working hard to help him. They went to the courthouse, the hospital, the wake, the funeral, and the cemetery. "What else do we do? He doesn't really care so much that his wife left. But he's devastated over his mother's and cousin's death. He won't talk about anything else when he's with us. All he says is 'Why did they have to die? They weren't old. They were just sick! Why didn't all of our prayers work? The doctors promised that they would both get well. Why did they have to die?' What do we do now?"

CAREGIVING WITH PERSONS WHO ARE BEREAVED

Most of us know someone who has lost a spouse, a family member, or a friend to death. That person could be a member of your family, a close friend, or might be yourself.

Caregiving with these persons may seem a bit more familiar than caring for someone who has lost his or her job. Yet, the care you give with these persons must be as carefully conceived and as intentional as the care you may give elsewhere.

Caregiving with these persons seems "easier" because you have seen this type of care given often in your communities. Florists advertise ways to care; funeral homes suggest appropriate responses; and churches practice this type of caregiving regularly.

Yet, many are unprepared to know what to do when they are the ones called upon to care for a person whose spouse, family member, or friend has died.

Remember that care does not end with the funeral for the one who has lost someone to death. Nor does it end when a few days or weeks have passed. The immediacy of the grief may be over after a few weeks;

however, the grieving process has just begun. Your care may be needed for several months and perhaps for years.

As in all cases, judge your responses in the light of "appropriateness." If your caring act feels appropriate, respond. If it does not, rethink your action. Also take your cues from the one who is grieving. He or she may truly need your caregiving early in the grief process, or he or she may actually need that care later. Or, you may or may not be the one who needs to provide ongoing care. Follow your instincts and ask others to help you decide what is appropriate and what is not.

As an Individual, You Might:

1. Personally visit at the funeral home, the church, the home, etc.
2. Express your concern with a card or telephone call.
3. Send flowers or a donation to a designated memorial fund.
4. Deliver food for the family during the days following the death and during the funeral.
5. Volunteer to help people sign the guest/visitation book during hours of visitation and during the funeral/graveside services.
6. Provide kitchen help for the family before and following the funeral (wash dishes, make lists of who brings food or flowers, etc.).
7. Return items (dishes, blankets, pillows, etc.) that may have been borrowed during the funeral.
8. Deliver paper goods to the home while there are guests (napkins, cups, plates, towels, bathroom tissue, etc.).
9. Help the person who is grieving with chores that must be done (lawn care, shopping, paying bills, auto maintenance, etc.).
10. Suggest persons to help with financial, legal, and other technical questions.
11. Offer to stay overnight when family and friends leave after the funeral.
12. Help with the children (carpools, transportation, child care, laundry, etc.). See also suggestions for caregiving with single parents, p. 11.
13. Invite your friend (and perhaps the children, if present) for a dinner at your home or at a restaurant.
14. Continue to call and send notes throughout the next year.
15. Pay particular attention to special days (birthdays, anniversaries, any other day that was special).
16. Provide opportunities for your friend to talk about the one who has died.
17. Ask how your friend is truly getting on, and listen carefully.

18. Give specific advice only when asked or only when the advice is desperately needed.

19. Invite your friend to attend social functions with you, and provide transportation both to and from the event.

20. Several weeks or months following the funeral, deliver flowers or a homebaked item unexpectedly.

21. Be a friend consistently and creatively throughout the first year or two following the death.

22. Keep your friend in your thoughts and prayers.

• *Add your own ideas here:*

As a Group, You Might:

1. Attend the visitation and/or funeral together.

2. Volunteer to provide for a complete meal(s) during the days following the death and the funeral.

3. If the one who is grieving has few friends or family near, offer to sit with her or him during the visitation and/or funeral.

4. Send a floral arrangement or make a contribution to a designated memorial fund.

5. Provide places to stay for family or friends who are attending the funeral.

6. Continue to include your friend in group activities, being sensitive to that person's need to separate from the group for a while.

7. Remove the name of the deceased person from mailing lists.

8. Remember important anniversaries or other dates that were important to your friend and express concern on those days.

9. Offer to sit with your friend during worship services, group functions, etc., so that she or he does not have to sit alone.

10. Find out if chores need to be done at the home of your friend, and divide those chores among group members.

11. Keep in contact with your friend and suggest appropriate support groups for persons who have lost family members or friends to death.

12. Keep in touch throughout the next several weeks, months, or years, and remain willing to respond as needs present themselves.

● *Add your own ideas here:*

As you care for persons who have lost spouses, friends, or family members by death, remember that grief is a very personal and private matter. Some of these persons will share their feelings with you, and others will not. However, that does not mean that grieving persons do not want to receive care from you. As you seek ways to care, listen carefully to the spoken and unspoken messages these persons send. Also, listen carefully to the suggestions from close friends and family members.

As you care for persons, help them talk about their understanding of the relationship God has to them during these days of sadness. At first, let them lead those discussions rather than sharing your own faith understandings. It may be appropriate for you to share your faith story, but be careful not to overpower the faith story of the one who is grieving.

Remember that consistent and thorough care is needed at any time when there has been a death. Also, remember to continue to care long after the funeral is over.

4. SINGLE ADULTS IN FINANCIAL CRISIS

Katherine slowly walked home from the bus stop. Shuffling steps moved her silently toward her basement apartment. Her general appearance suggested the feeling, "I'd rather go anywhere but home."

Her apartment has peeling paint, is damp and poorly lit, and is in the lower part of an aging building which has been condemned twice. With occasional bits of extra money, Katherine buys ivy and plastic flowers to decorate her few pieces of furniture. Most persons would run from such a "home," yet Katherine said recently, "My home is awful but it is my haven from the storm."

Katherine works two jobs. Each day she catches a bus at 5:30 A.M. and travels to a nursing home where she works as an aide. Backbreaking work awaits her each morning as she cleans and cares for the rooms and needs of 35 older persons. Following that job, Katherine quickly walks to a corner deli where she works as a cook and dishwasher. Arriving home about 11:30 P.M., Katherine falls into bed exhausted, trying to rest before she repeats her daily schedule. Neither job pays more than minimum wage and neither job offers a paid lunch break.

Financial trouble has plagued Katherine since her husband died fifteen years ago. Neither of them planned for the future, believing that they had time to save for retirement. Before he died, Katherine's husband was laid off from a local factory. The insurance and the pension which they once expected had disappeared. Soon after those losses, James complained of a heavy feeling in his chest. On the way to the hospital, he suffered a massive coronary attack and died, leaving Katherine with no means of support.

With family visibly absent during the funeral and the days that followed, Katherine decided that she would not ask anyone for help. "I can survive all of this! No one cares what happens to me."

So Katherine has survived—all alone. Her two jobs bring in just enough money so that she can pay her urban rent and buy groceries. Yet, she never has enough money for luxuries, "a new coat, winter shoes, a car, a decent haircut, a telephone, a delivered newspaper." Once a month, Katherine treats herself to an ice cream cone and a hamburger with fries. She has not had a vacation in fifteen years and expects none in the future.

Yet Katherine says, "I really am happy most of the time. Sometimes I notice how awful my apartment is, and sometimes I look in store windows and wish. But there's nothing I can do about that. So I just don't think about it very often, and I juggle the bills from week to week."

Asked what she would change about her life, Katherine says, "I wish I could go to school and learn to write so that I could be an author. I'd like to write novels. I'd like to visit New York City before I die, and I'd like to move out of this apartment and live in a six-room house with a picket fence. I'd also like to talk to children instead of have them run away from me. I guess I don't look good enough. These circles around my eyes must scare them away. What else do I wish for? Well, nothing—except I'd like someone to hug me sometime."

CAREGIVING WITH SINGLE ADULTS IN FINANCIAL CRISIS

To care for single adults like Katherine is hard work. Most single adults who are in financial crisis do not trust those who appear financially stable. Nor do they often trust institutions such as churches.

Yet the need to care for persons like Katherine is before us. We see single adults who are in financial crisis every day. For those of us who live in major cities, poor single adults are everywhere. Often, they are invisible to us—we may choose not to see them. Yet they live on our streets, often clean our offices or homes, or frequent our yard sales.

For those of us in rural areas, single adults who are in financial crisis often live at home with their parents. Others drift through our towns as they move from job to job. Still others live on our streets or in our fields. *And* they, too, are often invisible to most of us. Sometimes we know them by name but rarely pay much attention to them, saying "Oh, there's ol' Jack, the poor thing."

So, how do we care for these persons? We care with respect and with dignity. We treat these single adults with as much care as we would show our best friends. We do not jump in with caring acts—rather, we slowly determine what caring for a single adult in financial crisis means to that person. Sometimes, it means that we ask directly how we might care. At other times we listen for clues of ways to care.

Obviously, if a person is in a life-threatening situation, we must act more quickly. We would not leave a person in an unheated place in the winter when shelter was available. Yet, we must not force our care on someone who does not want our attention.

At times we don't know how to care. Yet, there are ways to care for single adults who are in financial crisis which are both respectful and which meet real needs. Here are some ideas for what both individuals and groups might do.

As an Individual, You Might:

1. Say hello when you pass someone on the street.
2. Spend some time talking and listening to the stories of the person's life.
3. Introduce yourself. Learn the name of the single adult.
4. Find out what you have in common and suggest some ways in which you both could interact around that common denominator, e.g., go on a picnic, walk in the park, listen to music, etc.
5. Suggest area community service agencies that can provide shelter, low-cost clothes, food, medical, or legal services.
6. Drop off a sack of groceries or toys for children.
7. Offer to help clean, paint, fix up an apartment, yard, car, etc.
8. Stay with the children (when present) while the parent has some time away.
9. Invite the single adult to your home for dinner.
10. Ask your friend to teach you a skill that he/she has, e.g., sewing, cooking, car repair, storytelling, etc.
11. Share your useable clothes and shoes with single adults or with agencies in the area which provide such to those in financial crisis.
12. Support with monetary gifts the local agencies which work with those in financial crisis.
13. Introduce your friend to someone who needs a new employee.
14. Provide tutoring lessons to those who cannot read well.
15. Offer to help your friend develop a budget that fits with his or her income.
16. Bring a flowering plant, a homebaked loaf of bread, a book, a newspaper, etc., when you visit in his or her home.
17. Invite your friend to go with you to church on Sunday or other church activities.
18. Talk with persons in your church about ways to create a more inclusive environment in your church. Talk about ways your church includes or excludes those in financial crisis.
19. Offer to pay for scholarships to camp for the children of those in financial trouble.
20. Offer to loan money very carefully. If you loan money, have an agreement for repayment or be sure that "a gift is a gift and not a loan."

● *Add your own ideas here:*

As a Group, You Might:
1. Talk about ways to make your group more inclusive and accepting of persons who are in financial crisis.
2. Study Bible passages related to what Jesus says about the poor and discuss ways you can respond.
3. Discuss reasons your group (or individuals in it) feels afraid of single adults who are in financial trouble. Discuss feelings about the story above. Talk about ways to interact with others so that the group can learn new ways to relate to those who may be different.
4. Provide for low- or no-cost activities so that all persons can participate.
5. Invite single adults who are in financial crisis to attend group gatherings.
6. Use the *Society of St. Stephen* material (see Resources, p. 105).
7. Talk with those in financial trouble about how they understand God and how they cope in a consumer-oriented city or nation.
8. Learn new ways to make gifts, cook, reuse items, etc.
9. Practice stewardship of money and resources. Share useable clothes, shoes, and other items with agencies which distribute these things to persons in financial trouble.
10. Support local, state, and national agency efforts to provide services to those in financial crisis. Lobby for assistance to those who are poor.
11. Provide tutoring services to adults and children who want to learn to read.
12. Offer low-cost child care for parents.
13. Provide a medical clinic for persons who need medical care.
14. Offer legal services or refer persons to low-cost legal services. Many churches have an attorney as a member who could assist with *pro bono* situations.
15. Provide shelters, food services, bath and laundry facilities, etc.

16. Work with Habitat for Humanity and their home building projects in your area. Offer carpentry services to persons who need repairs done in their apartments or homes.

17. Join with other churches or agencies to provide for some of the facilities and services listed above. Volunteer space in your church building for a shelter, a thrift store, food pantry, etc.

18. Connect persons who need jobs with employers who have positions available.

19. Offer job fairs or job counseling services.

20. Talk about when to refer persons for help. Have a list of referral agencies and services available.

• *Add your own ideas here:*

As you work with single adults who are in financial crisis, remember that you cannot change all of the conditions which caused the trouble. Yet, believe that you can make a significant difference in the lives of others. Your caregiving may be as "insignificant" as a smile or it may be as "significant" as helping someone find a better job.

Working with single adults who are in financial trouble, means being very careful to respond in ways that are not patronizing. Single adults in financial crisis have much to teach those of us who are more affluent. We can learn ways to live creatively with fewer resources and with less money. We can learn how to stretch dollars, how to buy less expensive food and clothes, and how to renew items that we might more often throw away.

As you care for single adults who are in financial crisis, believe that you will help a little and that you will learn a lot more. Risk learning about yourself and risk interacting with persons who may live very different lives from yours. Know that respectful and gentle acts of caring can make a significant difference in the lives of those who are experiencing both long- and short-term financial trouble.

5. SINGLE ADULTS RECOVERING FROM DIVORCE

Joseph and Sarah have filed for divorce. After twenty-eight years of marriage, both persons see no future for the healing of their relationship. Neither wants to cast blame on the other, yet both are bitter and distraught over recent happening in their lives.

After years of following Joseph's career from town to town, Sarah decided to go back to school in order to complete her business degree. At first, Joseph was thrilled by Sarah's decision. In fact, he willingly took over responsibilities for homecare and meal planning. Together they agreed that Sarah's primary work was to finish school and that she would continue to care for their financial matters. In addition, Sarah stated, "I really want to work in the garden. That's what helps relieve my stress, and, besides, I like a beautiful yard."

All went well for two semesters—or so they thought. However, Sarah became more and more involved in her projects at school. Returning home late at night became commonplace for her. As a result, Joseph quit making meals for Sarah. "I don't see any reason to fix dinner when that means that I have to refrigerate her meal night after night. If I'm going to cook, then I want to have Sarah here at dinner time . . . AND, I'm now having to mow the grass which I HATE doing because she's never here before dark to do it!"

Sarah acknowledged her part in the problem with Joseph, "I know I'm late almost every night. But I have to get my projects completed, and I need to work in the library where it's quiet. Joe always has the TV on, and I can't concentrate on my work."

Both Sarah and Joseph wanted to keep their marriage together, so they made appointments to talk to an area marriage counselor. Those meetings seemed to make matters better for a time. Summer passed, and both Joseph and Sarah believed that she could re-enter school for the fall semester without the problems that had plagued them the year before.

Two weeks after classes began in September, Joseph's boss requested a meeting. At that meeting, Joseph was offered the job he had always wanted—in a metropolitan area 850 miles away. Excited beyond his wildest thought, Joseph rushed home with the news. Upon hearing the words "a new job in . . . ", Sarah burst into tears. "What about me? What about my dreams? What about your promise that this time I could really finish school?"

After long hours of discussion, they reached a compromise—Sarah would stay to finish the remaining year and a half of school, and Joseph would move to the new job. Their friends said, "You're crazy! You'll never make it."

Yet for the next year and a half, Joseph and Sarah spent every available weekend together. "It's like we were on a honeymoon again. We were so glad to see each other that we forgot about any problems we had. We were both tired a lot, but we found a place to meet halfway between our towns. So, when we couldn't afford to fly for visits, we each drove part of the way."

At graduation, Joseph beamed as the proud husband of an honor student. Sarah announced at her dinner celebration following graduation, "And guess what!! I've been offered a wonderful job in . . . " Joseph's face crumbled as he realized that Sarah had no intention of following him to his town. Later he confronted her with his feelings and heard her say, "Joseph, I've followed you everywhere. Why can't you move to my town? It's a wonderful chance. I'll never have another one like it. I'm nearly fifty years old. Now's my chance, Joseph. Why can't you come with me this time?"

"I just can't. You know that, Sarah! You know how long I've wanted this job. I can't just leave it now and move off with no job in YOUR town. You know I can't do that. I can't imagine why you would think that I could. What's wrong with you? Why have you become so selfish lately? Can't you think of my career? I'm nearly fifty too. I just can't start over in a new town. Why don't you understand? Just find a job in my town and we'll be just fine."

"Maybe you'll be just fine, but I won't be! I can't do that again, Joseph."

So Joseph and Sarah have filed for divorce—not because either really wants one. They both say to their friends, their counselor, and their families, "We love each other. We just need to work in separate towns, and a commuting marriage just won't work for the long haul." Sarah continues, "It's not fair to ask either of us to give up opportunities that we both desperately want. And it's not fair to ask either of us to remain committed to a marriage when we do not intend to live together again. Retirement is a long time away. If it weren't, we might make it."

CAREGIVING WITH SINGLE ADULTS RECOVERING FROM DIVORCE

Caring for single adults who are divorcing calls for particular attention to the situation of each person. Each single adult who is divorcing has a different story, a different set of causes. Therefore, caregiving needs to be carefully tailored to fit the needs of each person. For example, in the story above, these two persons do not have children. Caring for them means that attention is paid primarily to the adults. In instances where there are children present, caregiving includes caring for the children and often the extended family (grandparents, aunts, uncles, etc.).

As a caregiver, you need to recognize that persons who are divorcing experience similar reactions to grief as do those who have lost a spouse to death. The grief process and the healing process are similar. Yet, there are very distinct differences. In divorce, "there is not a body to grieve over." Instead, grief often extends to the loss of a dream of a life lived as a married person, or to the loss of an image which others hold of the one divorcing.

In some areas of the country, divorce is more acceptable. As you seek to care for those who are divorcing, you may need to consider your own feelings about divorce. Or you may need to help persons in your town or church talk about their feelings. Where divorce is more common, those experiencing divorce may find ready support networks. In other areas, you may be called upon to offer or to create those networks of support and concern.

As an Individual, You Might:

1. Send a card or note expressing concern.

2. Call the person to ask what he/she might need from you (particularly if you are a good friend).

3. Offer a sympathetic ear. Listen to the stories about why the divorce occurred and to the stories about what life is like now.

4. Offer advice only if asked. Refrain from offering "You should have . . . ." or "You might have . . . ." Recognize that we don't need to add more guilt to the incredible burden which is borne by most persons who are divorcing.

5. Study the stages of grief and help your friend know that what he or she is feeling is "normal."

6. Find out where divorce recovery groups are located and invite your friend to participate in one. (Many groups are sponsored by churches, community service agencies, and counselors.)

7. Look at the suggestions for caring for the children of single parents (Chapter 2).

8. Give a good book to your friend. Most persons who are divorcing will read one book on divorce. Recommend or give a copy of one or two books on divorce or grief recovery to your friend. (See Resources, p. 105.)

9. If you have not experienced divorce yourself, read books and articles on the subject of divorce. Learn about the process of divorce (legally, emotionally, physically, etc.).

10. Recommend qualified lawyers, doctors, financial counselors, pastoral counselors, etc.

11. Study what the Bible has to say about divorce. (See Resources, p. 105 for suggestions.)

12. Recommend that your church consider its theological position on divorce. Read the Social Principles and suggest a church-wide study.

13. Invite your friend to attend worship services and other church activities with you.

14. Try not to take sides in divorce cases. Recognize that there are at least two different stories about the reasons for the divorce. Be supportive of both parties, if possible.

15. Recognize the pain and grief of persons who belong to the extended families or friendship circles of both parties. Offer support to these persons.

16. Understand that some persons who are divorcing may not feel a great deal of pain. Many persons have dealt with issues of the loss of their marriages long before the legal process has begun.

17. Offer to go with the person who is divorcing to the final hearing at the courthouse.

18. Remember special days which were important to the couple (birthdays, anniversaries, etc.).

19. If your friend is experiencing financial trouble, refer to the suggestions in the chapter, "Single Adults in Financial Crisis."

● *Add your own ideas here:*

As a Group, You Might:

1. Offer ongoing divorce recovery programs. (See Resources, p. 105, for help in starting a group.)

2. Study what the Bible says about marriage and divorce. (See Resources, p. 105, for suggestions.)

3. Discuss your theological position on divorce.

4. Discuss the story of Joseph and Sarah above. Talk out your feelings about each of the persons. Is divorce "justified" or reasonable in this case? Why or why not? Whom do you identify with and why?

5. Talk about ways to meet the needs of both parties in divorce. Usually one person in a divorce "gains custody of the church." How might your group reach out to both persons?

6. Invite your friends to participate in worship and other church activities.

7. Connect a newly divorcing person with another who has recovered from the trauma of divorce.

8. Provide a book service to those who are divorcing. Keep books available in the church library or deliver books to persons when you hear of impending divorce.

9. Have an up-to-date file of names of persons to whom divorcing people can be referred (lawyers, doctors, financial counselors, pastoral counselors, etc.).

10. Provide meals, clean the apartment, or run errands when a person is in early stages of divorce.

11. Offer to help your friend move.

12. Refer persons (adults and children) who may be victims of abuse to safe houses and to counseling programs.

13. Provide places where newly divorcing persons can find the supplies they need (dishes, sheets, vacuum cleaners, irons, etc.).

14. Offer to contact friends and relatives in cases of emergency. Provide hotlines for persons to call for help during divorce.

15. Provide a system in which others can trade services with each other; e.g., "I'll mow your grass if you can fix my car."

16. Offer opportunities for divorced persons to meet other adults in safe and caring atmospheres.

17. Provide low-cost, fun activities in which persons can participate with low levels of commitment expected.

18. Help divorcing persons practice ways to trust others, to make gradual commitments, and to gain confidence in themselves.

19. Offer acceptance and support to those who are divorcing. Work to be

nonjudgmental, yet help persons take responsibility for their part in the dissolution of their marriages.

20. Recognize that the counseling load for pastors in your church will increase as divorced persons become more comfortable at your church. Learn ways to provide for peer counseling. Provide for a supportive counseling network between staff and members of your group.

21. Offer classes or discussions on a variety of subjects (parenting, sexuality, financial management, Bible study, book studies, etc.).

• *Add your own ideas here:*

As you work with persons who are divorcing, remember that you cannot meet all of the needs. Yet, you can provide the support and care that many divorced persons are seeking. You can listen, provide healing networks of people and friends, offer places for persons to learn more about themselves and their relationship with others, etc.

Caregiving with persons who are divorcing should be tailored to meet the needs of individual persons. Caregiving CAN meet the needs of persons in groups. Growth and recovery often happens best when persons connect with each other. Therefore, offer places for networking and support.

Know that many persons who come to you for support are looking for affirmation of their own self-worth. Constantly hold before people the belief that all persons (single, divorced, etc.) are the children of a God who loves and cares for each of them. Break down the barriers in your town which insist that persons who are divorced are less worthy or worthwhile. Express in visible and vocal ways the fact that God's love extends to all people, regardless of their marital status.

6. SINGLE ADULTS WHO ARE YOUNG

Anita works as a clerk at a lawyer's office in a county seat town. She arrives at her desk daily at 7:45 and begins a similar routine. Anita describes her work as "boring, but it pays the bills." After an 8½-hour day, Anita quickly grabs a sandwich and runs off to her paralegal classes, three nights each week. For three hours a night, she crams information into her already tired brain. Finally home at 10:30 or 11:00, Anita jogs around the block to wake up and then spends about three hours studying.

On Saturday mornings you might find Anita doing her laundry, paying bills, jogging, and sometimes sleeping. "I'd rather sleep on Saturdays, but I'm getting fat. I've become a fast-food junkie. I don't have time to cook. Besides, I never really liked to cook. There's simply not enough time in each day to get all of this stuff done."

On Saturday afternoons, Anita makes time to see her friends "who think I've fallen in a well. They get mad at me because I don't have time for them. What they don't know is that I don't have time for myself. We go to the movies, rent video movies, eat out AGAIN, or just sit around." Sometimes her Saturday afternoon activities crowd into the evening. But usually Anita ends up at home on Saturday night, wondering "why I never have a date."

"I've had four dates this last year. My married friends tell me that dating is easy and that I should just find a man. Really!!! How do you find a man who isn't either weird or married or both? I have some very good male friends, but I don't date them. If I did, I would lose the only good friends I have. I wonder where you go to meet nice men. There aren't any at work, and the ones at school . . . well, I don't like any of them.

"My mother is pushing me to have a baby—after I find a man, of course! If she wants a baby so badly, I wish she'd have another one herself. She doesn't mean to hurt me, but I don't have time for a baby now. I can hardly take care of myself.

"My nextdoor neighbor at the apartment invited me to go to church with her. I tried it one Sunday, and now I can't get the preacher to quit calling me. He wants me to join the church. Why should I join a church here? I don't intend to live in this place forever, and I don't see any reason to join a church now. I wonder why I can't just go to that church as a visitor. Besides, I don't know what I believe, and I'd feel really fake if I walked down

31

there and said, 'I believe.' If I told my friends, they'd laugh. They know I don't know what I believe. Besides, I'm not good enough to join a church. I'm not married, and I have done some stuff that I know they think is wrong! They wouldn't let me visit if they knew. So I don't know if I'll keep going to that church or not. If my friends went there, I might."

CARING FOR SINGLE ADULTS WHO ARE YOUNG

Young, single adults are often missing from our churches, yet that does not mean that we should dismiss the responsibility to care for them, too. Typically, these young adults are between the ages of 20 and 30 (perhaps 35). Most have always been single, and most have some college education. Yet, some have not finished high school and feel very uncomfortable with those who have any type of diploma.

Caring for young, single adults usually means caring in very specific and personal ways. These persons are less likely to come to a singles ministry program, just as they are less likely to attend worship services. To care for them means, often, that we must go where they are rather than expecting them to come to us.

If we intend to care for young, single adults, we must learn what it means to be a "friend." These persons are looking for places where others know their names, and for experiences where they find meaning and significance in their lives.

Some young, single adults are divorced, and a few are widowed. Caring for these young adults calls for intentional efforts to attend to their feelings and thoughts. Most of them will not have peers who have experienced divorce or the death of a spouse; therefore, intentional caring acts may be extremely important if the young adult is to find solace and healing.

For young, single adults who have always been single, caring often means helping them connect with other single adult peers in healthy environments. Yet, many will not find support with older single adults whose life experience is greatly different. Therefore, caring for these persons may mean that you help to provide the social and friendship networks that they need.

As an Individual, You Might:
1. Consider what friendship means to you as a young single person (or what it means to your children, grandchildren, or friends).

2. Act as a friend even when your friendly acts are not reciprocated or when you do not receive "thank you's" or other expressions of gratitude.

3. Invite your friend to lunch. Make lunch appointments and pay the bill.

4. Provide a home-cooked meal occasionally.

5. Send birthday cards or special notes that let your friend know that he or she is remembered.

6. Call your friend to say "hello," or "I've been thinking about you," particularly if you have not seen him or her in a week or two.

7. Share your washing machine or dryer. Invite young, single adults to spend an evening every other week so that they can do their laundry and enjoy a visit.

8. Listen to stories about work, school, dating, and other activities.

9. Keep the stories of young, single adults confidential. Do not report those stories to parents, other friends, pastors, etc.

10. Visit young, single adults on college campuses, at their military bases or workplaces (where appropriate), etc.

11. Listen to stories about the lives of young adults—their experiences as children or youth, their feelings about their parents, their concerns about the future, and their worries about daily life.

12. Offer stories about your life. Help young, single adults know that you had (or have) similar experiences. Tell your stories in ways that do not sound like advice. Yet, be honest as you relate your experiences.

13. Help young, single adults understand the consequences of behavior (good or bad). Challenge behavior that is detrimental to their health or their emotional well-being.

14. If you see signs of depression or illness, refer these persons to qualified doctors or counselors.

15. Introduce your friend to other young adults and provide places for them to gather.

16. Suggest books or articles to read on subjects which may be useful, i.e., relationships, Bible study, job hunting, vacations, etc.

17. Invite your friend to attend worship with you. Consider other places your friend might like to go (museums, restaurants, parks, etc.). Invite him or her to go with you to these places, too.

18. Pray for your friend, and support the disciplines of prayer and Bible study that your friend may practice or may want to develop.

19. Encourage your friend to develop hobbies or take time to play. Help young, single adults to practice lifestyles in which work and studies are balanced with relaxation and renewal.

• *Add your own ideas here:*

As a Group, You Might:

1. Provide social settings (meals, parties, sports activities, etc.) in which young, single adults can meet their peers. Be sure to have food available at most group functions, particularly the social ones.

2. Suggest ways in which young, single adults can read and study the Bible with others and as a devotional time alone.

3. Discuss ways in which daily activities as lay persons connect with being faithful to God.

4. Help young, single adults struggle with what it means to believe in God and to live as disciples of Jesus Christ.

5. Connect the biblical story with stories of people in today's world (the young, single adults themselves and those persons whom they know or hear about through the media).

6. Provide places where young, single adults can talk about their reactions to current political, world-wide, economic, or other issues. Help them recognize their place in the world, and help them make connections between how their actions affect others in their cities, towns, nation, or world.

7. Provide places where young, single adults are known by name and where their absence is noted. Call them to say "we miss you." Visit them in their homes or workplaces, but be sure to call before you ring their doorbells.

8. Have birthday lists, and be sure that persons receive cards or calls on their special days.

9. Provide places to gather on holidays so that each young, single adult will not spend a holiday alone. Ask them to bring snacks, food, or other items to help make the day festive.

10. Go to movies together, read books in groups, play team sports, etc.

11. Connect young, single adults with children and persons older than themselves. Help them reach out to other generations in creative and mutually supportive ways.

12. Plan ways for young, single adults to make a difference in their communities. Provide ways for them to volunteer their services to build houses, provide tutoring services, staff homeless shelters or food banks, clean up neighborhood vacant lots, etc. Most young, single adults want to do these type of activities with others; therefore, plan ways to connect persons together for service.

13. Arrange times for young, single people to talk with their pastor(s). Help the young, single adults to think theologically. Help them know about church history and the traditions of your denomination.

14. Provide places for young adults to struggle with the social principles and attitudes of your denomination. Help them discuss their understanding of faithfulness as it relates to issues such as gambling, sexuality, pornography, addictive substances, war and peace, women's and men's roles, etc.

15. Create groups for study, play, worship, support, etc. Blend learning with fun, and help young, single adults struggle with their own faith concepts and beliefs. Help them know that all their questions are appropriate. Take seriously each discussion and be willing to search out answers together with them.

• *Add your own ideas here:*

As you care for young, single adults, recognize that each person has individual concerns and issues, and wants to be cared for individually. At the same time persons want places where they can interact with their peers and with those older or younger than themselves.

Find out where these single adults spend their leisure time. Go there, introduce yourself, and spend the time necessary to develop friendships.

Believe that the programs you develop for these young, single adults are less important than your individual caring acts. They want to get together with their peers. But they want to know that they as individuals are important to you.

Most important, as you care for these persons, remember that through your caring acts they can more fully understand what it means to be loved and cared for by God. Know that these young singles are adults who are developing and claiming their own beliefs about God through Jesus Christ. Through acts of caring and listening, help them make their own decisions about what it means to live as faithful children of God.

For young, single adults, caring ultimately means being a friend who walks with them as they make decisions which will affect their whole adult lives. Be patient, kind, and wise—not authoritarian—as you care for individuals and for persons within groups.

7. SINGLE ADULTS WHO ARE SATISFIED WITH LIFE

Lee finished his 10k run with a shout, "I did it!!!" Shouts of joy resounded as other people crossed the finish line. Lee exclaimed to anyone who would listen, "I made my life-long dream. Now I want to hike the Appalachian Trail from start to finish."

An outdoorsman, Lee rarely spends time inside. He is most happy when, after a day's work, he can change clothes and "hit the trail." When working as a consultant with state park construction and maintenance, Lee helps to lay out new hiking trails and recreation areas. Completely satisfied with his job, Lee tells his friends, "If I can do this job until I'm 80, and if my legs hold out for my running, I will always be happy!"

Divorced for seven years, Lee now cannot remember much about his unhappy days as a married man. He says, "Maybe I've blocked out all those fights and crisis moments, but I really don't remember them very well. I can't believe that it's only been seven years since my divorce. It feels like I've been single forever, and I love it!

"Sure I get lonely, but if I do, I just call up a friend and spend some time doing what I love to do best. I've got all kinds of women who want to spend time with me. Sometimes one of them wants to settle down and make a good arrangement permanent. I wish women would understand that I like being single. I don't plan ever to marry again. Why should I? I've got it all right now!!!"

Lee doesn't make a large salary, "but it's comfortable. I pay my bills and have money left at the end of the month. I save money each month so that I can quit my job in the next five years and hike the Trail. I don't know what I'll do after I've done that, but something will turn up. It always does."

Friends recently tried to get Lee to attend a singles meeting at a local church. Lee's response was, "Not me. I don't need them. They all talk about being single as if it were a disease. That's not for me."

Although Lee says publicly that his life is full and exciting, he does admit privately to a very special friend that he sometimes feels like he's missing something. That vague feeling of discontent never seems to emerge in a way in which Lee can discuss it. He describes the feeling as "a hole, a queasy feeling in my stomach, like butterflies when I was a kid about to speak in public." Because he can't define or describe the feeling,

Lee usually ignores it, believing that it "will go away, and it usually does. I feel it most often when I watch the news and see some poor person who can't find a job or a place to live. Sometimes I feel it when I think about being old. I wonder what my life will be like and I wonder if I will have done anything that truly mattered. But that's a long way away, so I don't think about it much."

What seemingly is most important to Lee now is his dream of hiking the Appalachian Trail. All of his attention is focused on that dream. His relationships with friends and family members are secondary, yet he describes those relationships as supportive and important. "It's okay for me to take off on a trail or to plan for the big Trail. They'll be here when I get back." A shadow crosses Lee's face as he says those words, and later he says that he hopes that his friends and family will be there then.

Emily is satisfied with her life. Working as a kindergarten teacher, Emily loves her relationships with children. Although she complains about the long school hours and various children who create classroom problems, Emily enjoys her work "with these kids. When they learn something, my heart soars. It's like seeing a flower bloom, especially when I've worked with one child who just couldn't get a concept and suddenly it makes sense. Sometimes I feel so much joy that I want to burst with excitement!"

A few years ago, Emily moved back home to live with her parents. "That was a hard time for us all, but I wanted to save money for a down payment on a house. The only way I could do that was to save money by living at home." Finally, there was enough money, and Emily bought a house. Artistic talent flows from Emily, and her house reflects the wide range of her creative decorating ability.

"I really like living alone. My house, the flower beds, and my dog keep me busy. I rarely feel lonely. I'm too busy with school, keeping current with new educational trends for children, walking Smokey, mowing the grass, weeding the flower beds, and doing all of those house things."

Emily rarely dates, although she has very close male and female friends. "I haven't met a man that's worth my time. That doesn't mean that I wouldn't like to date. I would! But where do you meet men? I'm not going on a search to bars or restaurants. That's degrading, and I haven't found a singles group that is very good."

Some friends say that Emily doesn't date because she is too shy and won't push herself to go to places where other single people meet. Others say that she has been badly hurt by past relationships and does not want to risk having that sort of pain again. Whatever the reason, Emily says, "Life is really all right. I'd like to marry sometime, but if I don't, I'll be fine. My life is full, and I'm content to keep living this way."

CAREGIVING WITH SINGLE ADULTS WHO ARE SATISFIED WITH LIFE

Outwardly these single adults appear as if all is well in their worlds. Often, that is in fact so. Many single adults are quite satisfied with their lives, their jobs, their relationships, and themselves. When asked if they would change anything about their lives, the answer is "no" or "probably not."

Caring for these single adults looks easy at first glance. Some might say they "don't need any care." Others might say, "I'll spend my time with persons who really need me." Yet, if you spend time with some of these single adults, you will often hear the haunting phrase, "there's something missing" or "I sometimes feel empty."

With other single adults, you will hear the comment, "I'm really happy and I want to share that feeling with others. I'm ready to give back to others what has been given to me."

As in all cases with single adults, caregiving cannot be prescribed in an easy fashion. Rather, caring means taking time to listen to the feelings, thoughts, and dreams of these persons. Caring means being available in the good times and the bad. For many of these single adults, life is so good that they rarely find the down times. Caring for these adults may mean that we stand with them in their daily experiences and challenge them to consider new ways to care for and serve the world around them.

As an Individual, You Might:

1. Talk to your friend and ask questions about how he or she views life. Listen carefully to both the joys and the stresses. Listen for those areas where there may be feelings of unease or curiosity.

2. Find out how your friend makes connections with other generations. Help connect your friend to children, youth, and adults who are older or younger. Many single adults, who feel satisfied with their lives, still long for connections with persons from different generations.

3. Discover what friendship means to these single adults as you interact with them. Challenge them to move beyond their circle of friends to become involved in the lives of others who may need their help.

4. Suggest that you and your friend volunteer in your community. Often these single adults want to do something that can make a difference in the lives of others; they simply need some encouragement.

5. Invite these single adults to join groups where the "meaning of life" questions can be discussed. Help them to put their lives and their faith into context with the rest of the world.

6. Introduce your friend to other single adults. Provide places where social connections can be made with various kinds of single adults. Challenge your friend to be concerned about and supportive of others whose life situations may not be as positive.

7. Look behind the façade that "life is wonderful" and listen for those places where these single adults need care and support.

8. Challenge single adults who are satisfied with their lives to give more of their money and time away to others. Help them see the connections between faithful stewardship of life and resources and their relationship with God.

9. Find ways in which these single adults can share their stories with others. Hearing about the experiences of others who see life as wonderful can be very helpful to other singles who are struggling with life.

10. Connect these single adults with married persons so that both groups can benefit from hearing about the positive nature of being single and being married. Many married persons cannot imagine that single life is full of promise and excitement. Help break down barriers of misunderstanding by providing for discussions.

11. Suggest to your pastor that these single adults could function as liturgists or other leaders in worship. Suggest that some of these persons may want to volunteer in other areas of the church's life.

12. Invite your friend to dinner, to a movie, for a hike, or other types of activities which you both enjoy.

13. Find ways to help your friend celebrate his or her life. Provide many opportunities for him or her to talk about daily experiences. In other words, be a friend.

● *Add your own ideas here:*

As a Group, You Might:

1. Offer various kinds of short-term educational activities which challenge and stimulate learning in various areas of life (faith, parenting, relationship building, current events, arts, finances, traditions from other ethnic groups or other countries, etc.).

2. Plan for retreats away from your town so that these single adults can focus on one topic for a length of time.

3. Provide ways for persons to volunteer with others. Develop work teams to build houses, tutor others, staff shelters or food kitchens, etc.

4. Develop group projects to raise money for causes. Help groups assess which agencies use gifts more wisely than others.

5. Contact denominational mission offices, your church's mission sending agencies, or other agencies to discover where a group might travel to provide service for others.

6. Offer social activities which connect persons with others in small and large group settings.

7. Discuss the use of group funds for activities such as ski trips, cruises, etc. Help these single adults determine for themselves how to spend money faithfully.

8. Discuss the social principles of your denomination. Help persons make choices related to their faith and the church's beliefs which are acted out in daily life.

9. Provide ways for single adults who are satisfied with their lives to celebrate their singleness. Plan a party or videotape group activities for a year and celebrate various accomplishments.

10. Offer a forum in which persons who are single and persons who are married can discuss their perceptions of each other. Through discussion, challenge participants to consider their stereotypes of others. Provide places for healing and acceptance to occur between single and married persons.

11. Discuss single people who appear in the Bible. What can those examples of God's people suggest for living as single people today?

12. Look at world leaders today who are single. Discuss how those lives can be examples for singles in your town.

13. Talk about the stress points during the year (holidays, days when the sun doesn't shine, etc.). Help these single adults to think about strategies for coping with days that aren't as positive as other days.

14. Help single adults who are satisfied with their lives consider what they want for their lives in the future. Talk about ways your group or the

church could help these adults deal with issues that will emerge in the future.

> • *Add your own ideas here:*

Caring for single adults who are satisfied with their lives is both fun and challenging. At first glance, these single adults do not appear to need care and support. Yet, caring is needed. As with any other single adult, these persons have stresses and uncertainties in their lives. At times they may create the illusion that "everything is fine in my life," but a careful listener can learn that specific acts of care may be needed.

Support and care for these single adults is most effective when the caregiver genuinely likes and is concerned about the other person. The word *friend* is the positive, satisfying symbol of care for this group of people.

As you interact with individuals and groups of these single adults, challenge them to care for others as well. Help them recognize that they are examples both to other singles and to married persons. Suggest that their very lives can be the images which will support and nurture the development of others. Ask them to care for you.

8. SINGLE ADULTS AT
RETIREMENT AGE

Charles celebrated his sixty-fourth birthday last month. Genuinely pleased with the surprise party that his office held, Charles has not been able to understand his sense of discomfort following this special day.

"I'm not tired, nor do I feel like I'm getting sick. I just feel strange— like there is something gnawing at my insides. I've never felt this way before, and nothing I do seems to make the feeling go away. What should I do?" he asked his friend.

This topic of conversation has repeated itself daily for the last few weeks. Charles has approached several friends, trying to figure out his sense of discomfort. In an effort to help him, two of these friends decided to have dinner with Charles in order to help him further explore his feelings.

Following dinner in a quiet restaurant, Charles began to explore his feelings, "I first felt this way three days before my birthday. I remember that day because I bought antacid tablets, hoping to stop the feeling in my stomach.

"On my birthday, I remember feeling excited and apprehensive all at the same time. I just thought the apprehension was related to being alone on that day. I really love my birthday, and my wife used to help me celebrate it so well. Then she died, and I've had to do the honors myself for the last few years. Oh well, you know, I've had friends help me celebrate, but it isn't quite the same."

That description seemed to give a reason for Charles' feelings for the days surrounding his birthday, but his friends were not satisfied. They kept pushing him to describe the next few days and weeks. What had happened, and how had he reacted?

"One day, I got a letter from the president of the company. Enclosed with that letter was an invitation to a staff meeting for those people who will be retiring in the next few months. I threw it away. I don't intend to retire for a few more years. I remember wondering why they sent it to me—I still wonder, I guess."

Charles' friends kept working with him for several hours, and finally all three concluded that his feelings of discomfort were directly linked to the letter from his company's president. Charles discovered in the conversation that he really was frightened that his boss would ask him to retire during the year.

Upon further reflection, Charles later decided that he was even more afraid of the hours that would face him after retirement. "What will I do with all of my time? I don't have a hobby, and my grandchildren all live hundreds of miles away. That big house will get bigger if I rattle around in it all day long."

As a result of these musings, Charles began to struggle aloud with friends about his dreams and fears related to retirement. He now sees some possibilities for action and is less afraid of approaching retirement. Although his boss has not set a date with him, Charles knows that the company president is expecting him to retire within two years. "That's better than what I thought he wanted. I've got some time to make some plans. I may travel. I might even move closer to my children and my grandchildren. I don't know yet, but it's kind of fun to think about what I might do. I still feel these twinges of discomfort, but not as often. I think they're related to this whole transition. At least the doctor said that they aren't something to worry about, and that helps relieve some fear about them."

Moving slowly, Lou touches all of her treasures in the living room. Sighing over some things, crying over others, and smiling still with others, Lou looks for the last time at many of the things she has collected for a lifetime. The movers are coming in an hour, and Lou will be leaving behind many of her treasured possessions.

Some items are marked "go," but most have the sign "stay" written haltingly on them. Lou has spent hours during this last week marking everything she owns.

Lou is approaching retirement, but hers is very different from that of Charles. After receiving the call informing her that there is a vacancy, Lou has had one week to decide what to take on her move to the retirement village located across the river. For Lou, moving to the other side of the river means moving to another world, to another part of life that she has dreaded for years.

"Oh, I know it will be okay, but this is home, and I'd rather stay here. But I guess these old bones need to move, and so I will." Lou and her daughter decided three years ago that Lou would move to the retirement home when she could no longer drive. Lou thought that day would never come, but last month it did. "I drove to the grocery store, I bought my groceries, and I went out to the car. All of a sudden, I didn't know how to get home. Now isn't that crazy? I've been driving home from that store for thirty-two years. I couldn't remember how to get back here. Well, I sat down and cried because I knew that I couldn't call Stephanie. She'd say, 'Mom, the time has come.' I know the time has come, but I don't want to leave this home. It's all I've known for so long. That place will be okay, but I don't know the people, and I won't know where anything is. And I can't take all of these treasures with me.

"You know, Sam died forty-four years ago—just when Stephanie started to junior high. I thought my life would end, but it didn't. She and I kept right on living. That's what Sam would have wanted. That's what wanted really, but I never thought today would come.

"Today's the day that I take two rooms of things. How do you decide what two rooms to take? It's like throwing away my own children. I love these things." So Lou moves from one thing to another, gently caressing each one. With tears streaming down her face, Lou says goodbye to her treasures—most of which will be divided among relatives and friends. Some items will be sold at an estate sale, and a few will be moved with her to the retirement village. "A retirement village? Imagine that!! I've lived long enough to go across the river. I wonder what Sam would say about that. He'd probably pat me on the back and say, 'Well, it'll be all right, Lou.' Maybe it will."

CAREGIVING WITH SINGLE ADULTS AT RETIREMENT AGE

Life is turned upside down when a single adult retires. All of the familiar routines and patterns of life are shifted and reordered. For some single adults, these changes are welcomed and embraced. Yet for others, retirement means painful separation from a part of life that has given meaning and significance.

Caring for single adults who are retiring means taking the time to listen for ways to care. As with all forms of caring, your acts of concern need to fit with the needs of the other adult. Pay attention to the words and to the behavior of the single adults who are retiring. Sometimes you will be told clearly what you can do to care. At other times, you may have to read the language of actions and behavior to gather clues for your caring. At all times, be appropriately respectful and generous with your concern.

Take note of who has provided nurture and support throughout the years. Talk with these persons to learn how you might care for the one retiring. If you are retired yourself, remember what acts of caring and concern were most helpful to you. Remember those that were not useful. Take your cues from your own experience. If you are not retired, talk to someone else who is. Learn from that person which acts of caring were most appreciated. What was helpful to one person may not transfer to another; therefore, choose your efforts carefully.

As an Individual, You Might:

1. Talk with the person who is retiring. Listen for places where caring might be appreciated. Remember that the most caring act for the person retiring may be your willingness to listen.

2. Attend the retirement party (if invited). If a party is not planned, talk to your friend about whether he or she would like a celebration. If so, plan a party and invite friends, family, and business associates.

3. Find out if gifts are appropriate. Many persons who are retiring do not want to receive gifts. If not and if you want to mark the retirement with a gift, find out what charity your friend supports. Make a donation in that person's name and ask that a notice be sent to your friend..

4. Help your friend move books, files, and other items from his or her office. If your friend is moving at the same time, help him or her pack, sort through items, or staff a yard sale.

5. Send a congratulatory card or flowers. Let your friend know that you remember him or her on the important retirement date.

6. Learn about the stages of grief and note how your friend is living with the grief associated with retirement. Help him or her talk about feelings related to the changes that are occurring.

7. Help single adults who are retiring to set some goals for the next several months. Suggest ways they can plan for both relaxation and for involvement in different types of activities.

8. If your friend likes the out-of-doors, plan an outing, play a game of golf, walk in the park, etc.

9. If your friend likes projects, help him or her with one—painting a room, cleaning the garage, enlarging a flower bed, waxing a car, etc.

10. Offer to water plants, take care of pets, or collect the mail when your friend goes on a trip or vacation.

11. Remember that the days immediately following retirement may be filled with activities and high energy. Be around for the slump that may come when the adrenaline rush subsides.

12. As with any loss, emotional reactions to retirement vary. Be avail-

able and supportive during various emotional responses following retirement.

13. At retirement, many single adults experience physical changes. Be aware of any symptoms that may emerge. If medical attention is needed, encourage your friend to visit a doctor.

14. Make telephone calls, send cards or notes, and generally let single adults who are retiring know that they are remembered often.

15. Suggest activities in which your friend might volunteer. Offer to volunteer with your friend.

16. Help single adults who are retiring anticipate changes in their lives—financial, physical, emotional, spiritual. Plan for ways your friend can meet these changes when they occur.

17. Talk about the significance of your friend's working life. Help your friend to celebrate successes and mourn failures. Consider how meaning has been found in living, and talk about ways in which God has been present throughout life. Discuss ways that meaning will be found for living in the future.

18. If your friend is not a member of a class or group, invite him or her to attend worship and other church activities with you.

19. Suggest books to read, places to visit, or hobbies to explore.

• *Add your own ideas here:*

As a Group, You Might:

1. Host a retirement party, a moving weekend, or a gathering for friends and family.

2. Talk in your group about the stories cited previously. How would you help these persons? Are there single adults in your area who are in similar situations? How might you help them?

3. Look at Bible passages describing persons who experienced significant changes in their lives as they grew older. How might these biblical stories support persons who are approaching retirement?

4. Talk about ways persons find meaning for their lives. If work activities or relationships have provided most of the meaning for persons'

lives, talk about how meaning for living will be found following retirement.

5. Create a scrapbook of letters from friends of the person who is retiring. Present the book at a party honoring the retirement of your group member.

6. Help persons make plans for their lives. Discuss ways persons continue to learn and grow following retirement.

7. Listen to and celebrate the accomplishments of persons who are approaching retirement.

8. Consider ways the whole church might honor persons who are retiring (articles in the church newspaper, bulletin boards, times during the worship service, receptions, etc.).

9. Discuss physical and emotional reactions to major changes such as retirement. Help persons anticipate some of their feelings so that they are not surprised by their reactions.

10. Recognize signs of stress or disturbance related to the changes accompanying retirement. Refer persons to physicians, counselors, etc., when necessary.

11. Develop peer support groups for persons approaching retirement. Plan ways for persons to talk about their feelings and thoughts before and after the date of retirement.

12. Suggest books or articles which relate to the subject of retirement or life changes in later years.

13. Help those retiring to recognize the changes that will occur in the lives of persons close to them. If single adults live near or with grown children or grandchildren, help them deal with the changes in the family structures that may occur following retirement.

14. Support persons who are grieving the loss of a job, relationships with those at the office, the daily routine of the working world, etc.

15. Invite persons to involve themselves in worship, group activities and social gatherings, volunteer programs, etc. Provide information about your group to local corporate personnel offices which handle retirees.

16. Connect persons together who have similar hobbies, interests, volunteer activities, etc. Persons who are retiring may need some support to find others who like to do similar things.

17. Provide social and fun activities that bring persons together. Consider taking short day-long trips to nearby museums, theaters, parks, etc.

18. Provide educational opportunities for persons who are retiring

(financial planning, health insurance seminars, setting goals for the next several months or years, reading circle groups, Bible study, faith-sharing groups, etc.).

• *Add your own ideas here:*

Single adults who are approaching retirement or other major changes in their lives look for the care and support of their friends, family, and church. Some of these single adults will need more attention than others. Yet, almost all will welcome persons who are willing to listen and to care in specific and appropriate ways. Most of the single adults are not "needy"; therefore, they are not looking for sympathy or for solicitous concern.

Yet, most do want to tell their stories about what it means to retire or to make major changes in their lives. Most want to consider what the meaning of their lives to this point has been. In addition, most want to consider ways to make the rest of their lives meaningful.

Single adults who are retiring usually are considering how they will spend their days. Many are searching for places to make a difference in the lives of others and in their community. Some well-connected persons do not need suggestions for places to volunteer, but others do need some ideas and would welcome persons willing to volunteer with them.

Single adults who are retiring do not necessarily have a "lot of time on their hands." Many have quite busy lives; however, some single adults find their lives empty and without a great deal of meaning. The former group may need support to unclutter their lives so that they can do those things that are most important to them. The latter group may need support to fill up their days.

Your role as the caregiver is to sort out where your help is needed. Listen carefully to the stories and clues your friends give you. Respond in appropriate and respectful ways.

9. SINGLE ADULTS WHO ARE FRIENDS

James recently celebrated his forty-third birthday, and his best friend, Sheila, took him to dinner. While at the restaurant, several of Sheila's friends from church were seated at a table nearby. Although Sheila attempted to say hello, her actions and words were ignored. Puzzled by their response, Sheila worried for a few days but then forgot about it.

The next week following Sunday school, Warren, Sheila's husband, met these friends in the hallway. All but one of them avoided him. One motioned nervously to Warren, "Come over here, Warren. I don't know how to tell you this, but Sheila is stepping out on you. We saw her at a restaurant with another man, and they looked like they were having a great time. I thought you should know. Let me know if you need to talk about it."

With as much control as he could muster, Warren said, "I know all about it. I don't have to explain Sheila's actions to you, and I'd rather you talk about this situation with her. But since you chose to inform me, I'll tell you: James is one of Sheila's dearest friends. I know and like James, and I'm glad she helped him celebrate his birthday."

His friend retorted, "Well, you must be blind to what is really going on. I could see that she's in love with the man. Why, they were laughing together and looked like they were telling each other all sorts of secrets. I know what we saw!"

"There is nothing going on except friendship, and I see no reason to try to change that. Besides, what business is this of yours?" replied Warren.

"Obviously, you don't know an affair when you see one. I feel really sorry for you. I think you could stop this now, and you might save your marriage. But, of course, if you don't care . . . ?" His friend's voice trailed off into silence.

Warren quickly ended the conversation and walked away to meet Sheila for worship. Following the service, Warren suggested that they go to lunch to "talk," and Sheila agreed. She had noted the cold feelings being expressed by her friends and was not sure what she had done to deserve such treatment.

At lunch, both Warren and Sheila recounted their separate experiences, and talked about their responses. Sheila has had several encounters with well-meaning persons who do not understand her friendship with James.

50

During lunch, she said again to Warren, "Other than you, James is my best friend. He's like the brother that I never had. I don't know how to convince people that what we have is a deep spiritual friendship, and nothing else is happening."

While Warren understood that statement intellectually, he admitted to Sheila that he did have lingering uneasy feelings, especially when he called from a business trip and didn't find her at home. "I know that you go to movies with James, and that's fine. But my old parental instructions say that's wrong. I don't know how to get rid of the feelings. I don't want you to give up your friendship with James, but this situation is creating some trouble for me, and, obviously, it's creating a great deal of trouble for our friends."

Warren and Sheila decided to continue talking with each other about their feelings and decided to explain their agreements to their friends. "But we may not be able to convince them. What if this gets all over the church? I don't want to be labeled as a woman having an affair! I'm not, but I don't know how to convince those people."

Later that week, James called Sheila to talk about a work project. Sheila decided to tell James about the situation at church. James did not take the news well. "Those busybodies! Why don't they mind their own business? We know that our relationship is right. You're like my sister, Sheila. I don't even think about you in any other way. I think all three of us need to talk this thing through. I don't want you to be caught in the middle, and I want to assure Warren that what you are is my best friend."

A few days later, the three sat down to a prolonged discussion about how each one felt and about actions they might take to relieve some of the tension that both Sheila and Warren were feeling at church. They agreed that this kind of discussion needed to occur frequently so that all three persons could express themselves. James said, "Besides, I'd like to be a better friend to you, Warren. Maybe the three of us need to appear in public together. Now, people will really talk about *that!*"

CAREGIVING WITH SINGLE ADULTS WHO ARE FRIENDS

Maintaining friendships with single adults is the most important caring act that other single persons and married people can express. The friendship connections between persons can be as strong as or stronger than relationships with family members. The friendship relationship is the key to healthy, lasting support and concern for another person.

Yet many single adults do not believe they can sustain friendships with others for long periods of time. Listen to these comments. "I lost my friends when I got my divorce." "My friends deserted me when my wife was sick and then died. I don't have any of those old life-long friends left." "When I got married, I lost my single friends." "Married people won't consider me as their friend. I guess I threaten their marriage or their relationship with each other. I don't mean to . . . I guess it's because of the myth that single people are 'wild and sex starved.' That's not true, but how do I convince them?" "If I'm a friend to a single person of the opposite sex, others think I'm dating or they immediately start asking about when the wedding date is. Why can't we just be friends without others trying to fix us up as potential marriage partners?" "If I'm seen too often with the same person, others think I'm involved in a homosexual relationship. My best friend is another man. Why shouldn't we go to movies together or go out to dinner together? Maybe I should wear a sign that says 'We're just friends!' It's getting to the point where you can't have a roommate of the same sex."

Caring as a friend to single adults requires intentional action and decisions. The culture pushes the single and married worlds apart, perhaps because so many marriages are fragile. Yet, most people know a single or married person who is or would be a wonderful friend. In some ways caring for single persons as friends means going against the stream of cultural belief and practice.

Of course we need to recognize the numbers of persons who have genuine friendships which shift slowly or suddenly into romantic involvement. Such entanglements between single adults and married adults will cause great pain. However, careful communication and responsible cultivation of friendship can avoid the blurring of a friendship into an affair. Friendships must be based on honesty and respect. On that basis, persons can develop relationships which transcend deception or unfaithfulness.

As an Individual, You Might:
  1. Talk about what friendship means to both persons.
  2. Talk about the ground rules for the friendship. What will you do together? What will you not do together? Friends have various expectations of each other. Make those expectations known.
  3. Be as truthful, honest, and open about your thoughts and feelings as possible.

4. Read books on elements of friendship and work to make your friendship even more supportive and positive.

5. If you are married, talk with your spouse about your single friend. Talk about your feelings, particularly those which may be uneasy. Discuss the ground rules you have set for the friendship. Always tell your spouse of any changes in your relationship with your friend. In addition, always keep your spouse informed of the plans that you and your friend make.

6. If you are single, talk about your feelings with your friend, particularly those feelings which may cause you discomfort. Remind each other of the expectations for your friendship. Always tell your friend if you experience any changes in your feelings about the friendship.

7. Recognize that others may have concerns about your friendships. Culture and morality are very closely intertwined. Talk with those whom you want to understand. Don't worry unnecessarily about those persons with whom you cannot talk or who will not change their opinions.

8. Suggest church-wide studies on the topic of friendship. Help to develop systems in which spiritual friends can be connected to other persons.

9. Learn what the Bible has to say about friendships, particularly those between Jonathan and David, Ruth and Naomi, Jesus and the disciples, etc. How can those biblical friendships inform the quality of friendships that you have?

10. Be attentive to the needs and concerns of your friends. Respond in the appropriate and caring ways suggested in other parts of this book.

11. Celebrate your friendships with others. Talk about why the friendships are so important. Discuss ways to be even more supportive and caring for each other.

12. Deal with anger, frustration, jealousy, or any other strong emotion quickly. Trust your friend to hear and to help you sort through your feelings.

13. Maintain the confidentiality of your friendship. Don't be tempted to gossip or to share information with others unless you have the permission of your friend.

14. Respect the needs for privacy and for commitment to other persons that your friend has. Expect your friend to respect your needs for privacy and for commitments to others.

15. Honor the dates for meetings that you have made with your friends. If "a better offer" comes along, talk with your friend about rescheduling or talk with your friend about the dilemma which you feel.

16. Recognize that all relationships change. Learn about ways friend-

ships mature and develop throughout the months and years. Your friendships will change as your life situations shift.

17. Recognize when you must leave a friendship behind. Learn about the stages of grief and know that you will experience similar feelings as your friendships end.

• *Add your own ideas here:*

As a Group, You Might:

1. Sponsor a study on friendship. Use examples of historical and biblical figures. Learn what made those friendships significant, and discuss ways those friendships can inform present relationships.

2. Plan ways for persons to consider not only their friendships with others but also their friendship and relationship with God. The connections persons have with God certainly influence the types of relationships they have with others. Help persons see those connections, and support persons as they strengthen their understanding of themselves in relationship with God and with others.

3. Apply learnings about dating relationships to your friendships. Many of the same communication and relationship-building skills that

are effective in dating also can be applied to the nurture of friendships.

4. Ask your pastor to include examples of single persons who are friends with married or single people in his or her sermons and prayers.

5. Suggest articles for your church newsletter which can include examples of friendship that transcend the marital divisions.

6. Explore with other group participants various understandings of friendship. Help persons consider their reactions to persons who are friends with married people, with same sex persons, with persons older or younger.

7. Link up people in ways that will support the development of close friendships.

8. Use resources which support the development of friendships. Read or study books on the subject of friendship. (See Resources, p. 105, for ideas.)

9. Offer multi-generational programs which help people of various ages meet each other. Support programs which intentionally connect single adults with people who are married, who are older or younger, etc.

10. Offer educational opportunities which help single adults to develop communication and relationship-building skills.

11. Suggest that participants in your program invite their friends to visit your group meetings.

12. Have a panel discussion on friendship. Talk about problems you encounter as you develop friendships with others. One panel participant might be a mental health counselor who can suggest ways to lower the threat level between friends and other persons.

13. Talk about feelings that harm friendships: jealousy, anger, fear, etc. Learn ways to deal with those feelings, and suggest methods persons can use to deal with those feelings.

14. Deal directly with persons in your church who may have negative feelings about friendships that develop between persons who are single and those who are married.

15. Talk with your pastor about including sermon illustrations which support the belief that being single is as valid a lifestyle as being married. Ask your pastor to suggest ways in which persons can bridge the gap between the single and married cultures in the church and in the community.

16. Support the development of marriage enrichment programs for persons who are married. Often when marriages are strengthened, couples become less protective of their relationship and are more accepting of friendships between spouses and single persons.

17. Offer dialogue sessions or a panel discussion between married and single persons. Use "friendship" as the discussion topic, and help persons explore various meanings of friendship.

• *Add your own ideas here:*

Friendships between persons are fragile gifts of God. Caring for single adults as friends means that you will nurture those friendships that persons have with each other. As a friend yourself, you can model high-quality friendships with others.

Help persons explore their conceptions about friendship. Plan ways in which those understandings can be challenged, can grow, and can change. Stand by those persons who are struggling with their friendships. Help others, who may be questioning certain friendships, to deal with their feelings openly and honestly, without making judgments on the friendships of others.

As an individual and as a group member, support programs which nurture the friendships of single adults. Help these adults to work not only on their friendships with others but on their friendship with God. Caring for single adults means providing ways in which the relationships between persons, others, and God can be nurtured.

PART TWO

Leadership for Single Adult Ministry Programs

*Advice, planning tools, and worksheets for leaders and workers with single adults.
"Beloved, since God loved us so much, we also ought to love one another. No one has ever seen God; if we love one another, God lives in us, and [God's] love is perfected in us"* (1 John 4:11, 12).

10. LISTENING

Each person and each church can be in ministry with single adults. Your ministry may be intentionally directed to individuals who are single, or you may choose to provide group settings in which ministry occurs. In addition, you may choose to combine both types of ministry for individuals and for a group.

Much of this manual centers the discussion on how persons can care individually for others. Descriptions for both individual and group acts of caring can be focused on the individual single adult. Many of you also want to develop or strengthen your group ministries with single adults. The following pages provide suggestions and instructions for that type of work.

Consider how the following ideas fit with your community and with your church. However, as you develop or strengthen your group ministries with single adults, do not forget to maintain your focus on caring for individual persons. Much attention can be paid to the maintenance of groups, to the detriment of individualized care and concern for persons.

Susan, Anita, Richard, and Marilyn recently met with their pastor to discuss their ideas for a single adult ministry program. They described their frustration with the singles restaurant and crowd scenes. They described their need for a Christian program which would include social activities and Bible study. They said, as with one voice, "We want a program, but we don't know how to start! We don't know where to meet, or what to do when we get together. Help!!"

What follows are learnings from their group and from other groups around the country. Various sections of material have been identified for your ease in finding the information that you most need.

These learnings and suggestions are not complete. You will have different experiences, but you will find that these ideas can grow and develop as you use them. As you begin your work, develop a way of keeping track of your learnings (the good ideas and the not so good ideas). Note how long it takes you to arrive at various places in the organization of your group. Keep notes on what works and what does not. Jot down the kinds of resources (people, books, etc.) that help you.

This information can be invaluable to you as you work to expand your program or as you "start over" after having planned some programs that didn't work. In addition, you can be very supportive and helpful to others in your community, district, or denominational networks which want to organize single adult ministry programs. Help others to know both the areas where your work went smoothly and also the places where there may be pitfalls.

CARING AS A GROUP FOR OTHERS

Before developing or expanding groups for single adults, consider how you can start now to be more intentionally in ministry with singles as individuals through your group efforts.

Each of us is asked to care for others. Frequently, the most caring act is the one of listening. As you read the suggestions in Part One of this manual, you probably noticed the frequent words, "listen carefully." Listening, truly listening, often is more important than other acts of caring.

Think about your own experiences when others have cared for you. What you may remember may be external acts of caring; however, those external acts were most likely accompanied by a person who listened. Maybe a person listened to things other than your words. Perhaps a friend noticed how you looked or acted. By responding to those cues, this person cared for your whole body and not just for your words.

Listening is ministry to others. All of us can learn to be better listeners. As you begin your plans for developing a group, start by learning to listen more effectively. If you have a small group working with you, plan a workshop and try to practice good listening skills.

High quality listening includes these elements:

- Paying attention to words, tone of voice, eye and body messages,
- Being available and visibly present to another person,
- Identifying the feelings that underlie the words of the speaker,
- Avoiding "thinking of what I'm going to say next" before the speaker finishes talking,
- Paying attention to what you are feeling as the other person speaks, your feelings may give you clues to how to respond,
- Asking appropriate follow-up questions so that you help the speaker talk further about his/her thoughts and feelings, and
- Responding to both the content of the words and the feelings.

Listening also means responding to what has been said. There are various ways to respond. Some responses are more appropriate than others. Consider what kind of answer is needed before you speak. Note these suggestions:

> Sometimes our responses to hurting persons suggest that we do not believe that they are capable of solving their own problem. When we give quick and easy answers, we often miss the real feeling that was behind the words. As a result, the person may resist us. Worse yet, our solution could be wrong for them. . . .
>
> Other responses reflect our need to get information rather than our need to identify with what the person might be feeling. It is helpful to ask ourselves how we would use the information. . . .
>
> At other times, our words are meant to offer reassurance. That is a natural thing for caring persons to do. But if reassurance is given too quickly, it may not be heard. Strong negative feelings may block hearing what could be altogether appropriate at a later time in the conversation. At other times, the person may not continue talking because he or she senses that we do not understand what is being felt or we do not think those feelings are very important. . . .
>
> Sometimes our responses indicate that we believe we can help another person deal with his/her hurt or loss through the use of logic. Logic tends to focus on words and not feelings. The result is that the person might well argue with us over the logic that has been used. . . .
>
> At other times our responses indicate that we want to avoid recognizing the person's feelings. When we do that, the implication is made that one should avoid life's difficult moments rather than deal with them in a faithful manner. . . .
>
> Other responses do not identify what the person is feeling but they do not carry the danger of stopping communication either. In a sense, the words are an invitation to say more. . . .
>
> Sometimes our responses get behind the words to get in touch with what a person is feeling. When that happens, there is a sense of being with the person who is hurting. . . .
>
> There are times when silence, a noncommittal response such as ('I see'), a touch, or a hug might be ways of being with a person and of encouraging him or her to continue to share with you (pp. 9-10, *A Ministry of Caring,* Duane A. Ewers, Discipleship Resources, 1983).

Listening can be a powerful ministry with single adults. Therefore, as you begin to develop your programs, continue to gain skills as a caring listener to individuals and to small groups of persons.

11. BEGINNING A SINGLE ADULT MINISTRY

As you follow this story of how one group is working to develop a single adult ministry program, pay attention to clues for planning. Woven in this story are key factors you will need to use when developing your activities.

After the conversation with their pastor, Anita, Susan, Richard, and Marilyn decided to continue developing a group for single adults in their church and community. They recruited another man to help them with their work. "We believe that we need nearly equal numbers of men and women on the planning team, if we can find volunteers.

"We also decided that what we are doing in planning is actually ministry for ourselves. Therefore, we begin each planning meeting with a short time of Bible study and prayer. We want to do what God is leading us to do, so Bible study is really important. Sometimes our pastor meets with us. At other times, she makes suggestions about passages we might discuss. We've learned that our needs are being met by meeting with each other. Oh, sure, we want to develop a group, but it's good to know that we can care for each other while planning for a larger group."

Following their devotional time, this group then spends the next hour and a half talking about what they have learned about their plans, what steps they need to take next, etc. "We started our planning process by working on what our vision for ministry is. That's hard work. It's easier to say, 'We'll just do a program on dating and the single adult.' Working on a vision for our work has really been important because we think God is guiding that discussion." A vision for ministry for this group includes these elements:

- Believing that what we want for ministry can happen,
- Changing our words into pictures of the reality that we want to create,
- Being positive about our ideas,
- Knowing that what we are doing will be exciting for others and that they will want to join with us to make it happen,
- Being aware that what we are doing will make a difference not only in our lives but also in the lives of others in our church and in our town, and

• Knowing that our vision statement will expand and change as we and as our program change.

"We made a commitment to work for two or three months on designing single adult programs. At that time, we want to be ready to go with something. We're not yet sure what that 'something' is, but we're getting a clearer image of that during each weekly meeting.

"Our plan for our work includes these topics for discussion, learning, and planning:

1. **"Find out what is happening in our town for single adults.** There's no reason to duplicate a good program that some other group is sponsoring. We also think that it's important to know what kinds of single adults are in this community." Are they divorced, widowed, single parents, always single people? Where do they go for support, entertainment, etc.? What is their economic and educational background? Where do they live, and how could we invite them to be a part of our group? (See Worksheet 1, p. 79, for a guide to determine information on single adults in your area.)

2. **"Find out what our church is offering for single adults.** Our church is not very big, but there are some activities here that we don't know about." What classes, groups, etc., invite single adults to participate? How does the worship service influence attendance by singles? What activities are sponsored for men and for women? What kind of child care will our church support?

3. **"Decide what group we are going to work with first.** We think that we're most likely to work best with people like us, but that leaves out a lot of other singles who would like to have a program here. But we think that we may try to meet needs of people similar to us first. Then, we can branch out to meet other needs.

4. **"Create a program that is exciting to us.** If we are bored by our plans, then we won't be very interested in inviting others to participate. So we think that we need to plan something that interests and challenges us.

5. **"Gain the continued support of our pastor.** She really wants us to succeed. She won't do our work for us, but she has been a real resource in connecting us to books, people, and ideas. Next, we need to gain the support of our Administrative Council. That group needs to agree with us that this ministry is important. We think that a few people will not be supportive, but most will. Some people don't think that single persons have enough in common to sustain a ministry. We're going to take a few

of these non-supportive people to lunch to talk about why a singles ministry program is important to us and why it could be important to them, too.

6. "**Find funds for our program.** We're not sure yet how much money we need, but getting into the church budget means that we are a bit more accepted by the whole church.

7. "**Create a six-month plan.** We want to kick off our program with a big party where we'll pass out a calendar of upcoming activities. We don't want a year's plan because we want to learn from others what they want to do, too. But we think that a six-month plan gives the message, 'We're doing something, and we want you to join.'

8. "**Develop a publicity campaign.** We know that without publicity, we'll never reach the people in town. We've recruited a single adult printer to join our discussion when we get ready to do publicity planning. He will do the printing for us at his cost. We're going to distribute the material through the mail and by door-to-door visits when we know where single adults live. We'll put material in the offices of dentists, doctors, counselors, bankers, and lawyers. We've already begun asking for permission to do that, and we haven't had one person say 'no.' We may do some radio and TV spots, but probably not at the first.

9. "**Divide up our tasks.** None of us can do all of this work. But we plan to recruit others to help us. That will help us find new people to come to our programs when we start them.

10. "**Start with a few, well-planned activities.** We can't do everything for everybody, but we can do a few things well.

11. "**Take care of planning group members.** We're really becoming good friends. We talk about our problems and frustrations at this planning process. But we know that we must take our time planning so that we start off with a good program. We're most afraid of doing all of this work and then not having anyone come to our meetings. We decided that if no singles come, we'd be upset, but then we'd just keep right on working on this idea. We really want a program for singles, and we believe that we're the ones who can do it!"

12. PROGRAMS FOR SINGLE ADULT MINISTRY

Various programs are offered across the country for single adults. Before we look at suggestions for programming, note these comments from another group.

"We think that all of our programs must include space for people to talk with each other. We encourage people to listen to each other, to ask questions, and to challenge each other when appropriate. We have offered classes to help people learn how to listen better. We have also trained persons in peer counseling support. Often single adults ask for advice and support, so we believe that our people need to have basic information about counseling and referral.

"We think that the most important part of our program is the way we connect people to others and to resources in the community and in our church. We also think that people are good resources for themselves, so we encourage them to practice self-disciplines which allow them to spend quiet time with their own thoughts and feelings. Through that process, we think it's also important for people to connect with God through Bible study, prayer, and worship.

"Our leaders help all of us think about how we serve each other. All of us can care for someone else. Even our single adults who are hurting the most can reach out to another person. So our program builds on those people connections.

"Networks are important, so we encourage people to talk with each other about all kinds of subjects. We've developed listening centers in which we learn where people would like to make connections, and then we link up people interested in similar topics.

"Social activities and service programs are very important. Not only do people want to have fun together, most people want to do something that makes a difference. So we develop programs which address both needs. We also offer places for people to learn and reflect on ideas and images."

No church or group can provide programs to meet every stated need. However, there are a variety of programs which groups of single adults have developed. Listed below are examples of these programs. When using these ideas, try to connect the kind of people you are serving with the type of program which will appeal to them. Develop a variety of programs so that broader audiences of single adults may be reached.

EDUCATIONAL PROGRAMS

Bible Study Groups: These groups range from studying specific books of the Bible to considering various words found throughout the Bible. Topics include Divorce and Biblical Ethics, Friendship and Biblical Characters, Jesus' Parables of Single Adults, etc. Some groups meet weekly. Others meet monthly. Some Bible study is done at retreats, during other occasions for gathering, and during small group meetings.

Sunday School Classes: These groups range in age from young singles classes to groups for older adults. Various topics are addressed, depending on the persons involved. Some classes are led by one teacher; others have a variety of teachers who are recruited by a class planning committee. Various materials are used, ranging from denominational curriculum resources, to books of general interest, to panels. Some groups use outside speakers while others use videotape and other multimedia resources.

Weekly Programs: Many groups gather weekly on a designated evening. Most programs begin with a fellowship gathering, followed by dinner, and a program. Various types of programs are developed, but most deal with issues of learning to live more effectively as a single adult. Topics range across Dating as a Single, Divorce Recovery, Learning to Communicate More Effectively, Vacations for Single Persons, Financial Discussions, and Volunteerism in the Community.

Retreats: Many groups organize yearly retreats. Some develop these retreats for the fall and spring. Others schedule them for times near holidays (New Year's, Thanksgiving, the Fourth of July). Some retreats are planned around a theme or a topic for study. Others are designed for fellowship and fun. (See Worksheet 5 and Worksheet 6, pp. 90 and 92, for sample retreat schedules.)

Resource Centers for Single Adults: Some churches have designated space in their library for books and materials related to singleness. These resources may be checked out, and persons are free to add to the resource center. Most groups have a person in charge of selecting resources and reviewing those which are donated.

Book Services: Some single adults have developed a book service which distributes books to persons who are experiencing a divorce or who have lost a spouse, family members, or friends to death. Persons deliver selected books so that others have available one or two helpful books to read on divorce, grief, or loss.

PASTORAL CARE

Counseling Services: Some churches or district denominational groups provide trained counselors who are available at sliding costs to single adults in the community or the church. Other churches rely on their pastoral staff to handle the counseling ministry. Still other churches train single adults as peer counselors, listeners, and caregivers.

Substance Abuse and Other Recovery Groups: Many churches offer space to various types of groups which deal with substance abuse: Alcoholics Anonymous, Narcotics Anonymous, Adult Children of Alcoholics, etc. Other churches offer space to programs which help sexual addicts, food addicts, those recovering from physical and emotional abuse, those who have been raped, those who have experienced a pregnancy loss, etc. Some of these groups are led by persons in the church. Most are led by groups organized within the community.

Referral Services: Many single adult groups provide referral systems so that persons can find agencies, people, educational programs, and resources within the community. Some groups develop referral brochures. Others provide bulletin boards or files of information.

Prayer Groups: Many single adult groups offer prayer groups for persons who want to learn about prayer and for those who want prayer partners or prayer groups.

One-to-One Support Programs: Some single adults have developed programs which connect individuals who are experiencing loss, trauma, or crisis with someone who has recovered from similar occurrences. Some of these programs are formalized in that they have designated persons who arrange the connections. Other groups connect persons through more informal means.

WORSHIP

Sunday Worship: Many single adults work regularly with their pastoral staff to make suggestions for creating more inclusive worship for single persons. Other churches use single adults as lay readers, liturgists, ushers, choir members, etc. Some worship services are more accepting of single adults than others. In these cases, various single adults meet with worship planners to recognize needs.

Teaching about Worship: Some single adult groups have organized programs which assist new members to learn about denominational worship. These programs provide opportunities to sing hymns and to learn about the sacraments, worship styles, the church year, etc.

Support for Prayer, Meditation, and Worship: Many groups actively support participation by single adults in worship services. Others teach and support persons as they develop their own styles of prayer and contemplative meditation. Retreats or programs on these subjects are held.

OUTREACH/SERVICE PROGRAMS

Mission Trips: Some single adults organize mission trips through Volunteers in Mission or other denominational and parachurch agencies. These trips take single adults to other locations and involve them in service to other people. Other groups organize local outreach programs, using programs such as Habitat for Humanity; local organizations which feed, shelter, and support the homeless; area tutoring programs, etc.

Referral Services: Many single adults want to help others across the world. Some groups make available information about places to send financial support, to volunteer individually, or to be a sponsor.

PROGRAMS FOCUSED ON LIFE CONCERNS

Parenting Groups: Some churches offer programs for single parents, helping them learn more effective parenting skills. These groups offer educational information and support for various life stages of the children and their parents. Some groups include ways to help children feel at home in church.

Divorce and Grief Recovery: Many single adults have organized divorce and grief recovery groups for persons experiencing recent divorce or the loss of a spouse by death. These programs range in length and format, but all are developed to support, guide, and enable persons to move on through grief to effective living as a single adult. In addition, some churches offer programs for recovery for children and youth whose parents are divorcing or whose parent has died.

Preparation for Marriage or Remarriage: Knowing that many single adults will marry for the first time or again, some single adult groups develop classes and programs for them. Some programs are weekend retreats. Others offer counseling for couples considering marriage or remarriage. Yet others provide workshops on ways to prepare for marriage, even if a wedding has not been planned or persons are not dating seriously.

Sexuality Issues: Classes, retreats, and workshops on sexuality and single adults are offered in many locations. These events help single adults consider their faith as they make decisions about their sexual expressions. Many groups use books, community resource persons, biblical material, and audiovisuals as resources.

Programs for Persons Who Cannot Attend Group Functions: Some single adults have developed visitation programs in area nursing homes, hospitals, prisons, etc. Some programs which include letter writing, visits, organized programs on bases, etc., have been developed with persons in the military services. Where possible, persons in military service are invited to attend single adult groups in the church or community.

FELLOWSHIP PROGRAMS

Meal Groups: Many programs are organized around meals. Dinners for Eight programs, Sunday lunch after worship groups, and holiday meal groups are examples.

Specific Programs for Men and Women: A few groups organize programs specifically for men or women. Some groups have an educational format, and others are designed primarily for support and nurture.

Sports and Recreation Programs: Various teams are organized which connect persons who want to play football, soccer, basketball, volleyball, etc. For those who do not enjoy team sports, other groups organize bike trips, hiking days, boating excursions, picnics, etc.

PROGRAMS FOR VARIOUS AGES

Church-Wide Activities: Many single adult groups support and sometimes sponsor all-church programs, retreats, dinners, parties, worship, and educational opportunities. Persons of any age and marital status are encouraged to participate.

Church Year Activities: Some churches sponsor special activities during special times: Advent and Christmas, Lent and Easter, Pentecost, etc.

These activities are usually developed for persons of all ages, regardless of marital status.

These are only a few of the multitudes of programs established in churches and communities. The scope and availability of programs is limited only by the persons who identify needs and plan for ministry with single adults.

Choices must be made. No church can effectively create all of the programs listed above. Your choices will determine the size and function of the group. Yet each church can develop some type of program for single adults. That program may be limited to one-to-one support and nurture ministries, or it may include a few group activities.

Whatever program is designed, remember to maintain the one-to-one connections between persons. Regardless of the size of the program, each single adult wants to be known by name and wants to feel a sense of belonging in your congregation. See Worksheet 4, p. 88, to assess which programs exist, which you need, and which should be dropped.

13. EXPANDING A PROGRAM

"'Singles Summit' began three years ago. We've done a lot of programs, and we've been successful. Now some of us are feeling bored and tired. Even the name we chose for our program seems old and outdated.

"Sometimes, we think we need something new to do, but we've thought of everything possible. Our new thoughts sound like retreads of things we've done before. . . . "

For some, expanding a program can re-energize a single adult program which seems sluggish. For others, expansion only means extending the life of a program which cannot be revived. In the latter case, a funeral may be needed for the old program. After the grieving for the old program has been completed, a new ministry program may be possible. New people can be recruited, and, along with a few oldtimers, new ideas can emerge for the beginning of new activities and ways to be in ministry.

However, a funeral is not always needed. Expansion of an existing program can provide new arenas for growth of continuing members and for visitors and new members. "But how do we get started in remodeling and expanding our old program?"

As you read the questions that follow, note both the questions and the answers to the questions. Woven in the answers are clues to suggestions for expanding your single adult program. The questions are posed so that you can structure a similar process for discussion of what you might do to strengthen or add to an existing program.

1. How did your program begin?

"We began our program for those who were newly divorced or for those who were dealing with significant loss in their lives. That program began when three persons who were going through divorce decided that they needed support from others in a similar situation. Our divorce recovery program is still going well for those people who are in the middle of separation and divorce. We really don't want to change that program. Soon after the beginning of our program for divorced persons, we began a program for the children of single parents. That program is doing well, too. Later, a group of persons who had lost a spouse to death began a program for widows and widowers. That group has stopped functioning, and so has our Friday night recreation bunch. The Friday night recreation group was never very strong. They had a difficult time getting people

71

to commit to attending the planned recreational programs. Sometimes, people would come in droves and at other times, no one came, so they stopped that program about six weeks ago."

2. What was the original purpose for your group?

"We wanted a program that would put people in touch with others who were like them. We wanted a group in which people could find support and nurture. We also hoped that they would find some support from God, but we were never very clear about how to do that. The group wanted to provide places for singles to meet other singles, and we hoped that the group would offer new ideas, a place to be cared for, and encouragement for the future."

3. How do you think you succeeded in reaching the purpose for the group?

"We reached it well as we developed these support groups for divorcing people and for the children of single parents. Those groups really do provide help for the people who participate. We never have figured out how to help people find support from God, and we certainly haven't reached very far into the single adult population in this town. We have a lot of work to do, but we really don't know what to do next."

4. Why do you think your program needs to be expanded?

"Well, those of us who have been part of it since the first are tired of it. We don't really need a support group for dealing with divorce. Those of us who have youth don't see a place for our teenagers in the group for children. We don't think the program is meeting our needs now. It did once, and it still does for those who are hurting badly from divorce. We need something new for us."

5. What are the things that you dream about for your future?
"Lots of things:
- Remarrying the right kind of person
- Sending my kids to college
- Taking a wonderful vacation with people I really like
- Doing something that helps someone else. I can't change all the hurts in the world, but I'd like to do something for someone else.
- Retiring in a few years. I'd like to feel like my life mattered. What I do now is fun and exciting, and I'd like to live that way in retirement."

6. How could the church help you realize these dreams?

"The church could help me think about what it would be like to remarry. I'd like to discuss what scares me about remarrying, and I'd like to talk to people who have. I particularly want to talk about how you deal with issues between children and a new husband."

"I need something to help me plan ways to save money for my daughter's college fund. She's only six years old now, but college will come. I can't count on her mother to contribute much toward that education, and if I don't start now, it will be too late. What I need is help in planning my finances and savings so that I can get the best return on my money."

"I want to take a vacation, but I don't want to go by myself. I wonder if the church could connect me with other people who want to travel. We could work out the details if I could find people who want to go."

"I work with paper and ideas all day long. Sometimes, I get home and wonder if any of what I did helped anybody. Usually my answer to that thought is 'no.' I'm troubled by the passages in the Bible that say, 'If you did it to one of the least of these . . . ' I don't know any 'least of these'— maybe I do—but I need help knowing how to care. I'd really like to get out and get dirty cleaning up a neighborhood, or I'd like to help a child learn to read. I'm not sure exactly what I want to do. I do know that I don't want to do that work by myself. I'd rather work on some project together with other single persons."

"I'll be retiring in a few years. I've had a good working life, and I'd like to have good retirement years. Somehow, I never thought I'd get old enough to retire. I guess the idea really scares me. I don't really have any hobbies. I can't imagine a life of leisure. What will I do all day long? I guess I'd like the church to help me sort all these feelings out and help me plan for a meaningful retirement."

You can ask similar questions.
- What do you worry about? How can the church help you deal with those worries?
- What are the stresses in your life? How can the church help you deal with those stresses?
- What are your hopes for the next two years, six years, ten years, etc.? How can the church help you deal with those hopes?

Following these questions, use a discussion and planning format which includes these questions:

1. From the suggestions of ways the church might help with these various issues, which idea would *you* like to work on?
2. From the suggestions of ways the church might help, which idea would *your group* like to work on?
3. Will this program or activity make a difference in the community of single adults? Will it fill a measureable need, meet a hope, etc., with single adults in the church and in the community?
4. Will some people in the church (the Council on Ministries/Administrative Council, the pastor, a few church leaders) support it?
5. Can the activity or program be described in ways that create visual images within the people who read your publicity?
6. Is the program or activity positive rather than negative?
7. Is the program achievable in a set period of time determined by the planning group?
8. Does the program invite others to participate? Does the program or activity invite new people? Does it fill the needs of a different group of persons than the ones who currently attend your programs? (Note: To expand your program, it may be necessary for you to develop new efforts which meet the needs of persons who are very different from those who participate now.)
9. Do you *really* want to do this program or activity?
10. Do others agree to take responsibility for the "who, what, when, where, how, and how much" questions? (See Worksheet 2, p. 85, as a handout for using these questions in a planning meeting.)

As you work to expand your programs, these and similar questions may guide your work.

In addition to using these questions, pay attention to the following suggestions:

- Pray for God's guidance as you work to expand your programs. Ask for clarity of purpose and for courage to risk new ventures in ministry with single adults.
- Publicize your programs in clear, concise, and attractive ways. Remember: You can never do too much publicity.
- Invite new people, your friends, persons whom you may not know well, business associates, neighbors, and others. Do not assume that

persons will come without an invitation. Most people attend a program because someone invited them.

- Recruit new people to be a part of your core planning group. As you recruit new leaders, your group will gain new ideas for creative efforts in single adult ministry.

- Constantly assess the needs, hopes, dreams, and stresses of the single adults in your community and church. As people's concerns change, so do your programs need to shift and grow to meet the issues of people in your community and church.

- Expand your program slowly. Adding new activities and programs can help your group grow, but adding too quickly can tire your planning group or leaders who have been recruited.

- Remember to provide some new large group activities so that single adults can gather with all the participants in the program. *And* remember to provide for small groups as well. Large group activities offer a sense that "we're all in this together," but small groups provide places for individual support and nurture among persons to grow.

- Compare your plans for expansion with your purpose for ministry statements. Make sure that your new programs support your purposes for ministry.

- Read *Five Audiences* (see Resources, p. 105) and work to develop programs which fit within the various audiences in the adult population. In addition, pay attention to the various audiences within the single adult population. Work to develop programs for various audiences (single parents, persons living through divorce or loss of a spouse to death, persons in financial crisis, those in other forms of crisis, etc.).

Expanding your programs can be challenging and exciting. Remember that you must make choices in ministry. As you remodel or expand your effort, do a few new things well. Leave some ideas to work on later. Refer some things to other groups who have the resources to develop those ideas into ministry efforts.

Most important, keep before you the images of your vision for ministry. Seek God's guidance and support.

14. RECRUITMENT AND CARE FOR LEADERS

Mary and James want to begin a single adult ministry program. They talked recently with their pastor, and he said, "I think you have a really good idea. Why don't you proceed with your planning and make a report to the Administrative Council next month." Feeling excited about possibilities, both Mary and James decided to follow these steps in developing leadership for the program:

"We're going to recruit three other people to help us. We know two women who will help, and James is going to find a man who will work with us. We need men on the planning group, and James does not want to carry all of that responsibility himself.

"We're recruiting these three people to help us for six months. After that time, we will ask these people to continue if they want. We also may need to recruit other kinds of people after six months. So, we're trying not to lock ourselves or others into a long commitment.

"Early in our planning, we want to discuss our expectations for our work. It's important for the people we recruit to know what we expect from their leadership. We also need to know what they expect from us.

"Also, we want to provide support for each other while we're planning. Both of us have been single a long time and feel comfortable most of the time. There are only a few days when both of us feel uncertain about being single. The three people we are recruiting have been single for a shorter period of time. So, we want our planning group to offer support to each of us. We know that our task is to plan, but we think we can balance that planning with caring for each other."

The conversations above suggest some keys to recruitment of leaders and offer some ideas for caring for leaders. Here are some additional suggestions.

- Talk about what type of leaders you need. Then look both within the membership of the church and in the community for those types of leaders. Remember, you may need to recruit leaders from the community for your single adult program. In fact, your program may grow by doing that!

• Recruit leaders personally. Visit in their homes, take them to lunch, or set a meeting following worship on Sunday morning. The best leaders are the ones you recruit personally. General pleas for help in the church newsletter or from the pulpit rarely give you quality leaders.

• Develop job descriptions so that persons know what they are being recruited to do. Set time limits as a part of those job descriptions. For example, recruit for three months a person to develop publicity for your program. Be as specific in your job descriptions as possible.

• After leaders are recruited, set times to talk with them about their work as leaders. Listen to their stories of frustration, joy, concern, and so on. Provide appropriate support and resources to help persons do their jobs well.

• Help the leaders you recruit to develop their own systems for support. Encourage them to recruit other single adults to help them.

• Set times to discuss learnings about single adult ministry with leaders. Make lists of learnings and evaluations of programs so that future leaders can gain help from current leaders.

• Provide for staff support of single adult leaders. Set times for volunteer leaders to talk with the pastoral staff. Discuss your visions for ministry, the successes or concerns related to the single adult program, and dreams for the future of single adult ministry at your church.

• Develop planning groups for single adult ministry. Some of these groups may be developed for short-term tasks. Others may be long-term councils or committees. Recruit leaders to staff these various groups.

• Evaluate the work of your leaders. Help them recognize their strengths and weaknesses as leaders. Provide appropriate training and support so that they learn to be even more effective leaders.

• Publicize the efforts of the single adult leaders. Tell stories of effective ministry done by the persons you have recruited. Help the church to celebrate the ministry that these persons provide for single adults in your community and church.

• Pay as much attention to caring for your leaders as you do for caring for members of your single adult group. Look for signs of fatigue or frustration. Encourage frequent meetings so that the leaders have opportunities to express their feelings, thoughts, ideas, and so on.

• Provide ways for the leaders of your single adult ministry program to grow in their own faith journey. Set time for Bible study, prayer, and reflection during your planning meetings. Remember that the spiritual growth of your leaders is more important than any task they may want to accomplish.

• Pray for leaders of your single adult ministry program. Encourage leaders to pray for each other and for single adults in the various groups within your church and community.

• Always look for potential new leaders. Persons that you recruit may get tired of their leadership responsibility. They may move to another town. They may marry or become involved in a significant relationship. They may want to serve as leaders only for a short period of time.

As a leader in single adult ministry, one of your chief tasks is the recruitment and care of other leaders. Take that responsibility seriously. Recruit and support the development of persons for leadership constantly. (See Worksheet 3, p. 87, to help you help leaders develop their leadership skills.)

One note of caution: As you work to develop and strengthen leaders, do not forget to find support and nurture for your own leadership. Ask for help—you can provide only so much leadership before you tire of "being the leader."

Make time for your own spiritual growth. Read the Bible and pray daily. Attend a small group where you aren't the leader—rather in that small group, strengthen your own understandings about God and faith.

WORKSHEET 1: DEMOGRAPHIC INFORMATION ABOUT SINGLE ADULTS

Use this form to determine who the single adults are in your community and in your church. If you know these measurements, you can begin to assess priorities and project the various costs of your programs based on estimating the numbers who will participate.

KNOWING MY COMMUNITY

(Much of this information can be obtained by contacting your public library or Chamber of Commerce. Ask for demographic data on single adults in your town, city, or county.)

The number of all adults who live in my town, city, or county _____

The number of single adults in my town, city, or county_____

The number of single adults between the ages of 19 and 30_____

31 and 55_____

over 55_____

(You may want to find out numbers of persons in the older adult age range. If so, determine your age brackets, and search for the information.)

The number of single parents in your town, city, or county_____

What opportunities are available for single adults in your area? Supply names of organizations and number of persons served on an annual basis:

Other churches:

Dating services:

Single adult clubs or other area singles groups:

Restaurants or night spots which cater to single adults:

Sports teams for single adults:

Other options for single adults:

Where do concentrated numbers of single adults live in your town, city, or county? Apartment or condominium complexes: (List the complexes closest to your church. Then list those farther away.):

Particular neighborhoods:

Other information which you may want to collect:

KNOWING MY CHURCH

(Your church records may have this information. If not, you may have to develop a survey or ask for approximate numbers.)

Your church's adult membership   _____

The number of single adults who are members   _____

The number of single adults between the ages of 19 and 30_____

31 and 55_____

over 55_____

(You may want to break the numbers of persons over 55 into categories.)

The number of single parents who have children under 18
living at home   _____

The number of single parents who have children under 18
who are living with another person   _____

List single adults in leadership positions in your church (for example,
Sunday school teachers, members of boards, committees, councils, task
forces, etc., members of the choir, etc.):

List existing programs for single adults (for example, classes, study
groups, weekday programs, visitation programs, activities for single parents, etc.):

What does your pastor think about single adult ministry? How supportive
is he or she? How important does your pastor believe singles ministry to
be? How will your pastor support your efforts in ministry with singles?

What do single adults in your church say? What are their needs, hopes,
concerns? How would they like the church to help them with these
issues?

What suggestions would they make for the kind of single adult program they would support? Who are potential leaders among these persons?

What did we learn?

What can we offer that is not already offered in the church or in the community?

What is our next step?

(For insights into planning ministry, see *Make a Difference You Can See: How to Plan for Ministry*, order no. DR049B, available from Discipleship Resources.)

TYPES OF SINGLE ADULTS

Here is a list of single adults who may be in your community or congregation. Can you think of others? How might you and your congregation be in ministry with some of these groups or individuals?

YOUNG—19-30

students
graduate students
professional/workers
single parents
divorced singles
widowed/widowers
financially troubled
those living as singles
    (spouses overseas/traveling)

runaways
homeless
separated
prisoners
unemployed/underemployed
emotional problems/mental or
    physical issues

MIDDLE—31-55

divorced
widowed/widowers
separated
single since birth
single parents (custody—non-
    custody)
unemployed/underemployed
professionals/workers
absent spouse
remarriage issues

prisoners
homeless
emotional problems/mental or
    physical issues
more women who are single
dealing with children leaving home
financially troubled
grandparents
students/graduate students

OLDER SINGLES—over 55

young olders
middle olders
older olders
frail olders
widows/widowers
divorced people
singles always
grandparents

professional/workers
retired
those in complex living situations
financially troubled
emotional problems/mental or
    physical issues
unemployed/underemployed

(Persons have unique needs and gifts. Always take care not to use these sociological categories as labels which define or limit a person's worth or wholeness in God's world.)

WORKSHEET 2: QUESTIONS TO USE IN PLANNING

1. What do you want for your life? What are your hopes? What are your dreams? What are your worries? What stresses do you feel?

2. How can the church help?

3. Do *I* want to do any work to address an idea listed in question 2 (the leader, a member of a planning group, an individual, etc.)?

4. Which idea listed in question number 2 do *we* want to work on?

5. Will a program/activity/effort make a difference in the community of single adults (will it fill a need, meet a hope, etc., with single adults in the church and in the community)?

6. Will the church support it? (Will a few "power" people support it? Does the pastor support it? Does the Council on Ministries/Administrative Council support it?)

7. Can I describe the program in a *word* picture? (Does the program description create mental images of what will occur at the program? If the program does not create mental images, it probably is not clearly focused.)

8. Is the program positive rather than negative?

9. Is the program achievable in a set period of time determined by the planning group?

10. Does the program invite others to participate?

11. Do we *really* want to do this program?

12. Do others agree to take responsibility for the "who, what, when, where, how, and how much" questions?

WORKSHEET 3: FOCUSING ON PERSONAL LEADERSHIP

What might I do
to develop my own
leadership?

What am I already
doing to build on my
own leadership?

What is something I
wish I could do but never
have time to do?

What do I want to do but
don't know how to do?

Are there resources available to help me?

How important is leader-
ship development in my life?

What two steps can I take?

With whom can I talk?

How will I know if I
have made progress?

What difference will
it make?

WORKSHEET 4: PROGRAMS FOR SINGLE ADULT MINISTRY

Educational Programs	*Exist*	*Needed*	*Drop*
Sunday school classes	( )	( )	( )
Bible study groups	( )	( )	( )
Retreats	( )	( )	( )
Weekly programs	( )	( )	( )
Monthly programs	( )	( )	( )
Short-term studies	( )	( )	( )
Issue study groups	( )	( )	( )
Discussion groups	( )	( )	( )
Resource Book Center	( )	( )	( )
Book Service	( )	( )	( )
Pastoral Care			
Counseling	( )	( )	( )
Substance abuse groups	( )	( )	( )
Prayer groups	( )	( )	( )
Referral services	( )	( )	( )
One-to-one care	( )	( )	( )
Support groups	( )	( )	( )
Worship			
Corporate worship	( )	( )	( )
Prayer groups	( )	( )	( )
Teaching about worship	( )	( )	( )
Church year activities	( )	( )	( )
Support for prayer and meditation	( )	( )	( )
Outreach			
Close to home/mission trips	( )	( )	( )
Referral and monetary support	( )	( )	( )

Programs Focused on *Life Concerns*	Exist	Needed	Drop
Preparation for marriage or remarriage	( )	( )	( )
Financial planning	( )	( )	( )
Sexuality issues	( )	( )	( )
Parenting groups	( )	( )	( )
Divorce and grief recovery	( )	( )	( )
Vocational choices	( )	( )	( )
Stewardship of life	( )	( )	( )
Social issues	( )	( )	( )
Groups for disabled persons, prisoners, families of inmates, nursing home residents, and military service persons	( )	( )	( )
Political action groups	( )	( )	( )
Neighborhood action groups	( )	( )	( )
Fellowship			
Meal groups	( )	( )	( )
Retreats	( )	( )	( )
Sports and recreation	( )	( )	( )
Camping/hiking/outdoor	( )	( )	( )
Men's and women's activities	( )	( )	( )
Small groups (e.g., Covenant Discipleship)	( )	( )	( )
Intergenerational			
Church-wide events and programs	( )	( )	( )
Sports and recreation	( )	( )	( )
Connections between generations	( )	( )	( )
Church year activities	( )	( )	( )

WORKSHEET 5: WORKCAMP WEEKEND RETREAT

Friday

6:00 p.m.	Arrive at campground
	Unpack
6:30 p.m.	Supper
7:30 p.m.	Group singing/group-building games
	TLC
	Divide into service teams
	Divide and load tools
	Bible study/reflection/set goals for weekend
	Worship
10:30 p.m.	To cabins
11:00 p.m.	Lights out!

Saturday

6:30 a.m.	Wake up
7:00 a.m.	Breakfast
7:30 a.m.	Circle up prayer
7:45 a.m.	Depart for work site(s)
5:30 p.m.	Return to camp
	Shower
6:30 p.m.	Supper
	Free time—volleyball, softball, soccer, football, frisbee
8:30 p.m.	Group singing
	TLC
	In service teams: Bible study, reflection on the day, total group sharing as desired
9:30 p.m.	Break—snacks
10:00 p.m.	Worship—leave as desired
11:00 p.m.	To cabins
11:30 p.m.	Lights out!

Sunday

6:30 a.m.	Wake up
7:30 a.m.	Breakfast
8:30 a.m.	Circle up prayer

8:45 a.m.	Depart for church school and worship at church of persons worked for
12:00 p.m.	Return to camp
	Lunch
	Pack, clean up
1:30 p.m.	Group singing
	TLC
	Evaluation—Did we meet our goals?
2:30 p.m.	Concluding prayer circle
	Depart for home

(Retreat model developed by Kathi Breazeale Finnell)

WORKSHEET 6: SPIRITUAL LIFE RETREAT SCHEDULE

No radios or tape players!

Saturday

1:00 p.m.	Arrive camp and unpack
1:30 p.m.	Group time I (Each group time will include singing, preparation for time alone, and a guided meditation.)
	Receive journal
	Guided meditation—Opening to God ("An Experiment in Listening," p. 58, *Journey Into Faith—Pastor's Guide,* Graded Press—resource for confirmation)
2:30 p.m.	Time alone I—Opening to God
3:30 p.m.	Group reflection/Sharing (Sharing will be in pairs, small groups, and total group)
4:00 p.m.	Break—Free time
	Swimming, hiking, volleyball, reading table of spiritual growth books
6:00 p.m.	Supper preparation
6:30 p.m.	Supper and clean-up
7:30 p.m.	Group time II—Nurturing Prayer and Praying the Scriptures (*Prayer, Stress and Our Inner Wounds,* Flora Slossa Wuellner, The Upper Room—chapter 2)
8:00 p.m.	Time alone II—Nurturing Prayer and Praying the Scriptures
9:00 p.m.	Group reflection/Sharing
9:30 p.m.	Break
10:00 p.m.	Group time III—Dreams/Darkness (*Dreams: Discovering Your Inner Teacher,* Clyde H. Reld, Winston Press)
10:30 p.m.	Time alone IIIA—Dreams/Darkness
11:00 p.m.	Night hike/Worship
Midnight	To cabins
12:30 a.m.	Lights out

Sunday

7:30 a.m.	Wake up
8:00 a.m.	
	Time alone IIIB—(Reflect on and interpret your dream if desired.)
8:30 a.m.	Breakfast and clean-up

9:30 a.m.	Group Reflection/Sharing of Dreams
10:00 a.m.	Break
10:15 a.m.	Group time IV—Prayer, Healing Inner Wounds (Wuellner book—chp. 6)
10:45 a.m.	Time alone IV
11:45 a.m.	Group reflection/Sharing
12:15 p.m.	Lunch preparation
12:45 p.m.	Lunch and clean-up
1:45 p.m.	Group time V—Practicing the Presence of God Each Day (Wuellner book—chp. 8)
2:15 p.m.	Time alone V
3:15 p.m.	Group reflection/Sharing in pairs or small groups only (Total group will share during 4:30 p.m. worship.)
3:30 p.m.	Free time
4:30 p.m.	Worship/Communion
5:30 p.m.	Pack and clean-up
6:30 p.m.	Leave camp

(Retreat model developed by Kathi Breazeale Finnell)

WORKSHEET 7: A PROGRESSION OF GROUP LEADERSHIP

An individual who has a dream and does something.

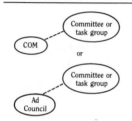

A committee (or task group) of concerned people who may or may not begin to relate to the Council Ministries (COM) or the Administrative Council (Ad. Council).

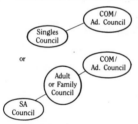

A council or task group that relates to the COM or Ad. Council or through an adult or family council to the COM or Ad. Council. This single adult council does all of the work, planning, and implementing the program.

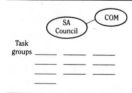

A council that develops task groups to do some of the work.

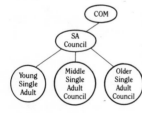

A council that develops specialized sub-units to do specific work for various audiences in the single adult population.

94

16. WHAT YOU WANTED TO KNOW

1. How do you find single adults who will participate in your programs? Most people attend group meetings because of five reasons.

First, single adults were invited by someone else. Most people respond positively to an invitation. "Come with me to _____."

By far, single adult groups grow best when members take responsibility to invite others, their friends, co-workers, neighbors, etc., to attend. More persons respond positively when someone says, "I'll pick you up so that we can go to _____."

Some churches have developed visitation programs in which members of the single adult group visit in pairs those persons who are prospective members for the group. These teams often choose one night a week for visitation. Visitors meet at the church for their assignments. They spend two hours visiting with single adults in their homes, apartments, condominiums, restaurants, etc. (Many of these visitation teams have made appointments before they ring doorbells.) Following the visitation time, the teams meet for coffee and snacks and discuss their learnings, feelings, and stories.

Second, single adults respond to publicity. Some people respond to advertisements in the newspaper. Others respond to visual invitations on bulletin boards, in brochures, etc.

When publicity is used, single adult groups follow various procedures. Most do monthly newsletters. Others develop special brochures which advertise various programs for single adults. These brochures are distributed in many ways—through lawyers', doctors', and judges' offices; through the mail to selected persons; through visitation teams; and through bulletin inserts during worship; etc.

Some churches pay for advertising in the area newspaper. Others buy space in local single adult community papers. Others use free time allotted to public service announcements on the radio or TV.

Whenever publicity methods are used, the materials need to contain these items:

- Clear messages—giving purpose of the program, time, place, dress required, babysitting available, cost, etc.

- Visual appeal—using color if possible and containing brief descriptions of the program.
- Descriptions of benefits to participants—suggesting ways the program will provide help with problems or concerns, information, ideas for living, contacts within the single adult population, etc.

Third, single adults initiate a call to the church when looking for a singles group. When they receive information, they decide whether or not to attend.

Every church office needs to contain specific information so that callers can be given complete and up-to-date news about your single adult program.

In addition, names, addresses, and phone numbers of persons who call the church can be given to single adults. These singles can call or visit persons who have expressed an interest in the program.

Fourth, some single adults are referred to your program by others. Some lawyers, mental health professionals, doctors, financial planners, and other community leaders refer single adults to churches. Anticipate such referrals by getting acquainted with these community leaders. Help them understand the ministry in which you are involved. Encourage them to refer persons to your program.

In addition, family, friends, and associates often refer single adults to churches where there are high-quality programs. Provide information to all church members about your program and encourage them to refer their friends and associates to your program. Ask church members for suggestions of single adults who might be interested in your activities. Spread the word about your ministry to every person in your congregation. Make recruitment of new members a priority not only among singles but also among others in your church who do not participate in your program.

Fifth, some single adults walk into your building looking for a singles program. These persons often attend worship first, or they may arrive at the Sunday school hour. Be alert and be looking for visitors who are single. Provide single adult greeters to the Christian education program who know how and when to direct visitors to your group.

Whenever your group meets, designate persons to watch for visitors. These designated people need to:

- Be friendly!

- Invite the visitor to sit with him or her.
- Introduce the visitor to other persons in the group.
- Learn something about who the visitor is so that caring can begin immediately.
- Make certain that the visitor fills out a card, giving name, address, and phone number.
- Be sure that this card is given to the persons who are committed to call or visit the visitor within a few days.
- If worship or other activities follow your group meeting, invite the visitor to go with you to that function.

2. How do we plan for single adult ministry within small membership churches?

Not every small membership church has enough resources to provide for an ongoing single adult program. But every church, regardless of its size, can provide for one-to-one acts of care and concern. Each church can practice using many of the suggestions found in Parts One and Two of this resource.

All churches, from the smallest to the largest, must make choices in how they provide for ministry with single adults. In small membership churches, you may not be able to provide for a program, but you can respond to crisis, or needs for personal friends. In addition, you can make certain that your worship services and church programs are inclusive for single adults. For example, encourage your pastor to use examples of single adults in sermon illustrations. Recruit single persons to sing in the choir, to serve as lay readers, or to help serve communion. For church programs, you can make certain to invite single persons to 'church-wide' picnics rather than 'family night suppers.' Or you can provide child care for single parents during church meetings.

Some persons work together to develop district-wide or county-wide programs for single adults. Some of these programs are ecumenical. Others are planned by leaders within the United Methodist or other specific denominations. Some of these programs meet monthly. Others meet more frequently. The key to effectiveness within these programs is found in the continuity of the program. They meet at the same time and in the same place. All the participating churches share as equally as possible in the cost (money and volunteers) for the program. The pastors work to support these activities and are not threatened when participants choose to visit other church services on Sundays. Leaders for the program are carefully chosen, and each leader is given specific tasks to do.

New leaders are recruited constantly, and persons work hard to invite single adults in the area to participate.

3. How do you recruit men to participate?

Many men actively participate in single adult groups. But many more do not. You can raise the attendance and commitment levels if you provide specifically for men and their interests.

Men attend when there are other men present. The numbers of men and women do not have to be equal. However, your program needs to reflect the presence of men. You may want to recruit men to be greeters, to make announcements, and to participate on your planning committee. (Try to achieve equal numbers of men on your planning committee. Establish men as visible leaders in both planning and leadership at group functions.)

Recognize that some men do not enjoy discussion formats. Provide a variety of programs which may include retreats, outdoor activities, sports, programs which include their children in play and quality time, short-term studies, conferences, workshops, service projects in the community, trips (socials, service, etc.). Pay attention to the special needs of men: stress at work, feelings of loss with children living away, loneliness, issues of finding significant relationships with women and other men, questions about finding meaning for life, and health issues.

In order to develop male attendance at your meetings, you probably need to recruit men from the community to join your activities. Do not rely only on the male members of your congregation. Remember to invite men from the community specifically to functions of your group. Do not give generic invitations, "We hope to see you sometime." Rather, make specific invitations. Describe the program and its benefits to men.

4. How necessary is child care?

Child care is critically necessary for parents of preschool and elementary age children. Some persons will choose to participate in your programs if you have child care, and they will stay if you don't. In addition, keep the price for your child-care provisions low, since many of these adults are already paying large sums for day care. Provide meals for children when parents have meals served.

As you plan for children, remember to keep the quality of your programs high. Single parents expect excellence in activities for their children and will not participate in your single adult activities if their children are not provided with stimulating experiences, especially since they may be appropriating valuable personal time with a child in order to participate with your adult program.

Consider offering programs which deal with issues of loss related to divorce or the death of a parent. Provide ways for children to deal with these issues in various levels, ranging from talking about their feelings and thoughts to expressing those experiences through art.

Plan programs which help children do their homework or which support their learning during the summertime. Offer programs which nurture the development of children's faith.

And do not forget to offer high-quality times for play and recreation. Many of these children need the release that only play can afford.

During the summer, consider offering activities during the day so that parents can have options for child care during working hours. In addition, you might develop summer programs in which children and parents can participate together in joint programs.

Do not forget to offer similar high-quality programs for the youth of single parents. Plan programs which range widely from fun and recreation to significant ways to deal with anger, frustration, and loss of trust when dealing with parents who are divorcing.

5. Can you mix ages of single adults?

Sometimes you can mix the ages. However, remember that single adults range in age from 18 to 80 and 90. The life issues and concerns of this vast age span create difficulty if you attempt to offer programs for all of the ages.

Yet, there are significant ways in which you can combine ages in programs so that persons have ways to learn from other singles of an age very different from their own.

Many persons under thirty see themselves as "not yet married." Therefore, they have very different issues from those persons who are recovering from divorce or traumatic loss of other types. In addition, persons over sixty-five often do not think of themselves as single either. They use words such as *widowed* or *older adult*. Sometimes they claim the word *single* but more often they do not.

You may consider planning for the middle-aged group of singles between 30 and 55-65. These persons mix well together, regardless of the reasons for their singleness. Most persons who have always been single at age 35 have had significant losses in their lives. While they cannot relate to the specific trauma of divorce, they can understand the feelings of anger, loss, emptiness, and depression.

In addition, these single adults have similar concerns that are related to work issues. Many are dealing with similar issues of aging parents, raising children, dating, etc.

One idea to consider in mixing the ages is to combine ages in fellowship or social settings and in short-term service or study. Recognize that even some of these activities need to be planned for part of the population, rather than combining all of the ages together. Plan for ongoing programs that address the specific needs of more narrowly defined age groups.

6. **What can you do for socially inhibited single adults?** At times, you may find your group attracting a few (often several) single adults who are socially inhibited. That is, they lack the social skills needed to relate effectively with others. Some of these persons can learn the social skills necessary. Others may need to be referred for counseling or for treatment services.

Consider the size of the group to determine how you respond to these persons. A larger group (15 and up) can absorb one or two socially inhibited persons. If you are attracting more of these persons, you may want to develop a program specifically designed for them.

Or you may want to work with the larger group to learn special ways of relating to these persons. In addition, your group members can practice caring specifically one-to-one with these persons. Many of the suggestions found earlier in this book may help you define adequate strategies for ministry.

Some groups work to recruit these persons to perform special functions in the larger life of the church, i.e., answering the phone on Sunday mornings, working in the church gardens or lawn, working with the nursery children, etc.

Most groups eventually must consider confronting persons who lack necessary social skills. These confrontations must be carefully designed and must present love, concern, and support for both the person and for the group. Set boundaries for appropriate behavior, establish limits of ways in which persons can participate in the program, and refer persons to effective places where skill development can be practiced and learned. In all cases, work with others to create strategies for appropriate and loving responses to persons who are socially inhibited.

7. **How do you enlist support of church leaders?** Do your homework and establish a case for single adult ministry. Show numbers of single

adults in the church and in the community. Relate how single adults are already involved in the ministry and life of the church. Create visions of how single adults can be even more related to the Christian faith and ministry of your church.

Do research (both formal and informal) to learn stories of single adults and how ministry through the church can help these persons in their daily life as they seek to commit their lives even more to faithful living. Link the social life concerns of single adults with the larger concerns of finding meaning for life.

Pay attention to the social principles or particular beliefs that church members have related to moral and ethical issues. Work with church leaders to help them see their place in ministry with single adults who are also growing in their understanding of appropriate ways to live.

In addition, create strategies which recognize "who's in power" and how those persons can support your efforts in single adult ministry. Carefully select key leaders and take them to lunch (or dinner or meet with them following worship) to talk with them about your vision for ministry with single adults. Recruit them as supporters of your program and of your vision for ministry.

You **must** have the support of your pastor(s). If your pastor does not support your program or your ideas for ministry, you will have difficulty sustaining your ministry. If you are having trouble convincing your pastor of the importance of ministry with single adults, talk together about his or her reasons for not supporting your plans. Work to be open and friendly in your conversations. Anger and frustration will not help you gain his or her support. If the reasons are based on theological or biblical images, work to present your ideas for ministry which are based in other understandings of theology or biblical images. Help your pastor see your ministry as a program which supports and loves the church, the Bible, and faith.

In addition, do not leave to a few persons the responsibility of convincing leaders in the church of the need for single adults. Recruit many people to help you with this task. Also, work with others in your group to help them understand the need for active and loyal support of the church's program and ministry. It's hard to ignore persons who attend worship, give generously of time and money, and respond positively to other church programs!

8. **What do you do if your program doesn't work or you lose members?** First, celebrate your successes, and don't be discouraged! Second, assess

the parts of your ministry strategies which are working well and consider which ones are not. Third, try again and again. Do not give up on the first few attempts to establish a group. Often, programs take several months (perhaps even one or two years) to get started and well established.

Assess the needs of single adults in your community and in your church frequently. Needs, hopes, and concerns change in the lives of single adults. Programs that worked well for a while may need to be shifted or changed as life issues of persons change. Don't be afraid to drop a program which is no longer meeting needs.

Recognize that the audience you are trying to reach may not be an audience with which you can work effectively. For example, if a majority of single adults are attending a large church in the area, you probably will not want to plan a program for the persons who attend those functions. Consider other audiences which may be attracted more to your church than to the large one nearby.

Consider your recruitment plan for leaders. The leaders you recruit will attract persons similar to themselves. If your leaders are not exciting and inspiring persons, you may have trouble attracting others to join your program.

Evaluate your plans for ministry. Look at your action plans. Did you follow these plans well? What worked in your plan and what didn't? Consider also the way you implemented your plan. Did persons who were responsible for carrying out tasks do their work well? Do you need other leaders to carry out those plans, or are your current leaders adequate?

Recognize what you have learned from your efforts. What could you do differently? What would you change? Where would you like to work next?

Remember that programs go through cycles. Single adults often move from group to group. Because your group once thrived and now doesn't, this doesn't mean that it will never thrive again. Refocus your efforts, support your leadership, and begin new programs. Programs need to change as people change. Again, do not be afraid to stop some programs in order to begin new ones.

Focus on your relational ministry with single adults. Know that the way you care for persons may be more effective and meaningful than all of the programs you could sponsor. Certainly, single adults want to participate in programs with other singles. But most persons will respond positively when they know that their particular concerns and needs are being addressed in one-to-one acts of caring. In other words, keep your focus on people and not on numbers of participants.

9. **What happens when leaders marry, move, or quit?** Celebrate the leadership of those who leave. Help others to see that persons in leadership are valued and appreciated. Develop an environment in your program in which leadership is respected and valued. Support your leaders in visible and verbal ways—not just when they leave, but frequently.

RECRUIT, RECRUIT, RECRUIT!! An ongoing, sometimes frustrating job is recruitment. But the nature of ministry with singles suggests that, as the lives of singles change, so do your leadership requirements. Recruit personally. Do not rely on newsletters, appeals from the pulpit, or general announcements that "we need leaders."

Plan rotations for leaders. Recruit them for six months (a year maximum). Avoid using "career" singles, those who have been single for a long time and are bitter. Many persons who have always been single will be wonderful leaders, but those who are angry or disappointed will not be.

Pair leadership so that persons work together to fulfill tasks. Paired leadership also means that leadership for programs continues even if one of the pair leaves or quits.

Support your leaders. Recognize their talents for leadership. Thank them for their efforts. Remember their birthdays and celebrate their achievements. When you recruit leaders, work with them. Do not leave them alone to fulfill their tasks. Provide staff support from the church (typing, mailing, calling, etc.).

Train your leaders. They may not have skills to lead groups, but you can help them plan agendas, assign tasks, and follow up on efforts of others. Train persons by shifting them from short-term tasks to longer tasks. Do not ask a new leader to take on responsibility for a huge task immediately. Move persons from smaller tasks to larger ones. Send persons to training events for leaders in single adult ministry in your area. Or plan for leadership training to be held in your church.

Consider the gifts and talents of members. Recruit persons for leadership based on their talents or skills. Do not ask persons to do something in which they are not interested.

Maintain a core of leaders. Your program needs to depend on many persons, not just on one personality. Shift persons in and out of the core of leadership. Support the core leadership to recruit others to do tasks as well. The core leaders need not take all responsibilities for leadership. Others can be recruited too.

Reconsider the direction for the group. Encourage new leaders to change and adapt the single adult program to meet their images for the group and for ministry with single adults.

10. **Do we need a singles council?** Some groups function best with a council. Others work better with a committee or task group. (See Worksheet 7, p. 94, for a chart which describes the leadership progression for a group.) When making a decision about a council, ask these questions:

- What leadership do you need for your program?
- Will an organized, structured council facilitate the leadership for your group? Will a council structure hinder your work?
- Consider where your program and leadership are in relation to the chart on Worksheet 7. What structure do you need to help you develop your program?
- What is your pool of potential leaders? Can your church's single adult program support the number of leaders needed on a council? On a task group? On a committee?
- Have you talked to your pastor and other key leaders about the type of leadership group the overall church will support?
- Think of other questions that will help you decide.

Note: The number of persons needed on a council will vary depending on the size of your program. Most singles councils range between 8 and 15 members. Some groups have organized structures with officers and established committees. Others work in a more fluid way, recruiting council members to do various tasks throughout the year.

Most councils rotate members so that about one-half of the group remains on the council in any given year. Councils which rotate all of their members at the same time have trouble maintaining continuity of their work.

Terms on the council are determined by the group. Some groups rotate members on an every-6-month plan. Other groups ask members to serve for one- to two-year terms. Some groups nominate their own new members. Others work with the nominations and personnel committee for recruitment of leaders.

Most groups create their leadership teams or councils slowly. When a program is new or developing, less structured leadership is needed. As the group ages and expands, the organization of a singles council becomes more important.

11. **List other questions here.** Look for answers in this book and in other resources. In addition, consider how you might discover answers to your questions from persons in your community or church. Ask people to help you with your questions.

RESOURCES

Listed below are resources for individuals and for leaders in single adult ministry programs. This list is not an exhaustive one. Resources for single adults and for leaders in programs change frequently. Check your local bookstores or denominational resource centers or catalogs for the most up-to-date resources.

FOR THE CAREGIVER

Aging and Single Adults

Aging: A Time for New Learning, David J. Maitland. John Knox Press, 1987. Suggests ideas for expanding knowledge and personal growth as persons age.

American Association of Retired Persons, 1909 K Street N.W., Washington, D.C. 20094. Contact this office for their resource lists.

Faith for the Older Years: Making the Most of Life's Second Half of Life, Paul D. Maves. Augsburg Press, 1986. Contains suggestions for building a vital faith throughout life.

Mature Years, a quarterly publication of The United Methodist Church to help persons in and nearing retirement years. Order from Cokesbury Service Centers.

Vintage Years: Growing Older with Meaning and Hope, William E. Hulme. Westminster Press, 1986. Provides ideas for finding meaning and hope as persons grow older.

Teaching Older Adults: A Guide for Teachers and Leaders, Linda Jane Vogel. Discipleship Resources, 1988.

The Gift of Maturity: New Images for Older Adults, Chester E. Custer, Editor. Discipleship Resources, 1986.

Divorce and Single Adults

Crazy Time: Surviving Divorce, Abigail Trafford. Bantam Books, 1984. Passages or "crazy times" that persons survive as they rebuild life as single adults.

Creative Divorce, Mel Krantzler. The New American Library, 1975. A classic guide to the stages of divorce and recovery.

Marital Separation: Managing after Marriage Ends, Robert S. Weiss.

Basic Books, 1977. A practical guide to divorce and its process, including theory and personal reporting.

Marriage and Divorce: What the Bible Says, James M. Efird. Abingdon Press, 1985. Suggests a United Methodist understanding of biblical material related to marriage and divorce.

What to Do When Your Son or Daughter Divorces, Dorothy Weiss Gottlieb, Inez Bellow Gottlieb, and Marjorie Slavin. Bantam Books, 1988. Practical help for parents, grandparents, and other family members.

Grief and Loss

But I Never Thought He'd Die, Miriam Baker Nye. Westminster Press, 1978. A guide to recovering from the death of a spouse.

Good Grief, Granger Westberg. Fortress Press, 1962. A classic guide to understanding the stages of grief and grief recovery.

The Grief Recovery Handbook, John James and Frank Cherry. Harper and Row, 1988. Step-by-step suggestions for dealing with loss.

How Do We Tell the Children?, Dan Schaefer and Christine Lyons. Newmarket Press, 1988. Guide to helping children understand and cope with death.

How to Survive the Loss of a Love, Melba Colgrove, Harold H. Bloomfield, and Peter McWilliams. Bantam Books, 1981. Provides ideas and helps for persons experiencing any kind of loss.

Necessary Losses, Judith Viorst. Fawcett Press, 1987. Helps persons recognize the loss of loves, illusions, and expectations in order to grow as adults.

Rebuilding, Bruce Fisher. Impact Publishers, 1981. A guide for persons as they rebuild their lives after any significant loss.

Starting Over: Help for Young Widows and Widowers, Adele Rice Nudel. Dodd, Mead & Co., 1986. Contains practical suggestions for young single adults whose spouses have died.

General Resources

Adult Children of Alcoholics, Janet Geringer Woititz. Health Communications, Inc., 1983. Provides information and support for the adult children of alcoholics.

The Angry Book, Theodore Issac Rubin. Collier Books, 1969. A classic guide to dealing with anger appropriately.

Do I Have to Give Up Me to Be Loved by You?, Jordan Paul and Margaret Paul. CompCare Publishers, 1983. Explores the nature of committed and lasting relationships, with useful hints for dealing with conflict.

Famous Singles of the Bible, Brian L. Harbour. Broadman Press, 1980. Describes biblical characters who are single.

How to Be Your Own Best Friend, Mildred Newman and Bernard Berkowitz. Ballantine Books, 1971. Suggestions for learning to be a friend to oneself.

How to Forgive Your Ex-Husband and Get on with Your Life, Marcia Hootman and Patt Perkins. Warner Books, 1985. Contains ideas for dealing with feelings of anger and resentment in order to live effectively as a single adult.

The Hug Therapy Book, Kathleen Keating. CompCare Publishers, 1983; *Hug Therapy 2,* Kathleen Keating. CompCare Publishers, 1987. Provide a humorous look at persons' need for hugs and touches.

The Joy of Being Single, Janice Harayda. Doubleday and Company, 1986. Lists ideas persons can use to feel whole and creative as single adults.

Just Friends, Lillian B. Rubin. Harper and Row, 1985. Discusses the role of friendship in persons' lives.

Living Alone and Liking It!, Lynn Shahan. Warner Books, 1982. Provides useful suggestions for enjoying life alone.

Preparing to Marry Again, Dick Dunn. Singles Ministry Resources (P.O. Box 1472, Roswell, GA 30077). Discusses information related to remarriage.

The Road Less Traveled, M. Scott Peck. Touchstone Books, 1978. Discusses concepts of love which build whole relationships.

What Color Is Your Parachute?, Richard Boles. Ten Speed Press, 1988. A manual for jobhunters and for those who are considering job changes.

When All You Ever Wanted Isn't Enough, Harold Kushner. Pocket Books, 1986. Guide to finding joy, meaning, and purpose for living.

Why Am I Afraid to Tell You Who I Am?, John Powell. Tabor Publishing. Helps for self-awareness and interpersonal communication.

Sexuality Resources

Male Sexuality, Bernie Zilbergeld and John Ullman. Little, 1978. Provides information for men regarding sexuality issues.

For Yourself: The Fulfillment of Female Sexuality, Lonnie Garfield Barbach. Doubleday, 1975. Contains information for women regarding sexuality issues.

Single Parents

Being a Single Parent, Andre Bustanoby. Pyranee Books, 1985. Helps for raising children alone.

The Boys and Girls Book about Divorce, Richard Gardner. Bantam Books, 1988. Provides honest and reassuring answers to questions about divorce.

Help Your Child Learn Right from Wrong, Sidney Simon and Sally Wendkos Olds. McGraw-Hill, 1977. Value formation suggestions for parents.

How to Talk So Kids Will Listen and Listen So Kids Will Talk, Adele Faber and Elaine Mazlish. Avon Books, 1982. Communication guides for parents and children.

The Kids Guide to Divorce, John Brogan and Ula Maiden. Fawcett Crest, 1986. Suggestions for children aged 11 and up.

Latchkey Children and Their Parents, Lynette Long and Thomas Long. Arbor House, 1983. A complete guide for children and working parents.

Mothers and Divorce, Terry Arendell. University of California Press, 1986. Explores legal, economic, and social dilemmas of being a single mother.

Parents, Please Don't Sit on Your Kids, Clare Cherry. Lake Publishers, 1985. Guide to non-punitive disciplines.

Self-Esteem: A Family Affair, Jean Illsay Clarke. Harper and Row, 1980. Suggestions for building self-esteem within the family.

Single Fathers, Geoffrey Greif. Lexington Books, 1985. Provides information and support for single fathers.

Two Thousand and One Hints for Working Mothers, Gloria Gilbert Mayer. Quill Books, 1983. Great suggestions for mothers and others in the home.

Spirituality and Discipleship Growth Resources

The Bible Makes Sense, Walter Brueggemann. John Knox Press, 1977. Help for understanding the Bible.

The Bible Speaks to You, Robert McAfee Brown. Westminster Press, 1985. Suggestions for reading the Bible.

Celebrating the Single Life: A Spirituality for Single Persons in Today's World, Susan Muto. Doubleday and Company, 1982. Thoughts of claiming the gift of singleness.

Each One a Minister, William J. Carter. Discipleship Resources, 1986. Suggestions for persons who want to live out their faith in daily life.

For Everything There Is a Season, Karen Greenwaldt. The Upper Room, 1988. Meditations for single adults.

A Guide to Prayer for Ministers and Other Servants, Rueben P. Job and Norman Shawchuck. The Upper Room, 1983. A guide for daily prayer and meditation.

How to Meditate, Lawrence LeShan. Bantam Books, 1986. A guide to self-discovery.

Lifesigns, Henri Nouwen. Doubleday and Company, 1986. Suggestions for learning how to deal with fear in order to live intimately with God and others.

Prayer, Stress, and Our Inner Wounds, Flora Slosson Wuellner. The Upper Room, 1985. Suggestions for dealing with inner feelings in order to live more effective lives.

Reaching Out, Henri Nouwen. Doubleday and Company, 1975. Ways to learn the three movements of the spiritual life.

Unexpected News, Robert McAfee Brown. Westminster Press, 1984. Reading the Bible through Third World eyes.

The Way of the Heart, Henri Nouwen. Ballantine Books, 1985. Uncover power through prayer, solitude, and silence.

Weavings, Vol 2., No. 4., July/August, 1987. Discusses spiritual friendship.

FOR THE LEADER

Developing Compassion

A Ministry of Caring, Leader's Guide and Participant's Guide, Duane A. Ewers. Discipleship Resources, 1983. A process for learning skills for caring.

AIDS and the Church, Earl Shelp and Ronald Sunderland. Westminster Press, 1987. Suggestions for the church's ministry with persons who have AIDS.

AIDS: Faithful Witness on Today's Issues. General Board of Church and Society of The United Methodist Church, 1990.

Burnout—The Cost of Caring, Christina Maslach. Prentice-Hall Press, 1982. Recognize, prevent, and cure symptoms of burnout.

Comforting Those Who Grieve, Doug Manning. Harper and Row, 1985. A guide for those who care for others, with helps on grief recovery seminars.

On Death and Dying, Elizabeth Kübler-Ross. Collier Books, 1969. A classic guide for understanding the stages of dying and grief.

Tear Catchers, Harold Ivan Smith. Abingdon Books, 1984. Suggestions for caregivers.

The Wounded Healer, Henri Nouwen. Image Books, 1979. Suggestions for those who would care for others in today's world.

Developing Spirituality and Discipleship Growth

Covenant Discipleship, David Lowes Watson. Discipleship Resources, 1991. A handbook for Covenant Discipleship groups in congregations.

The Art of Biblical Narrative, Robert Alter. Basic Publishing, 1981. Suggestions for doing Bible study.

Companions on the Inner Way, Morton Kelsey. Crossroad Books, 1983. Suggestions for spiritual guidance.

The Different Drum, M. Scott Peck. Touchstone Books, 1978. Helps to build a sense of community with all the world.

Forming Ministry Through Bible Study, Robert Paul. Discipleship Resources, 1988. Suggestions for leading Bible study.

A Guidebook for Spiritual Friends, Barry Woodbridge. The Upper Room, 1985. Suggestions for those who want to strengthen their friendships with others.

Opening to God, Carolyn Stahl. The Upper Room, 1977. Guided meditations and suggestions for leaders.

Spiritual Friend, Tilden Edwards. Paulist Press, 1980. A guide for those who wish to provide spiritual direction.

Divorce and Grief Recovery Resources

Divorce Recovery Workshop, Leader's Guide and Participant's Guide. Doug Morphis. Discipleship Resources, 1986. Manuals for leaders and participants in seven-week programs for divorce recovery.

Doorways: Living Through the Death of a Spouse, United Methodist Curriculum Resources (Graded Press), Cokesbury Service Center. A curriculum resource for helping those who have lost a spouse to death.

Doorways: Living Through Divorce, United Methodist Curriculum Resources (Graded Press), Cokesbury Service Center. A curriculum resource for helping those who are divorcing.

Doorways: Living Through Separation, United Methodist Curriculum Resources (Graded Press), Cokesbury Service Center. A curriculum resource for helping those who are separated from their spouses.

Marriage and Divorce: What the Bible Says, James Efird. Abingdon Books, 1985. Suggests a United Methodist understanding of biblical material related to marriage and divorce.

Uncoupling, Diane Vaughan. Vintage Books, 1986. Discusses why relationships come apart.

General Resources

The Challenge of Single Adult Ministry, Douglas W. Johnson. Judson Press, 1982. Suggestions for building a single adult ministry program.

Children of Alcoholism, Barbara L. Wood. New York: University Press, 1987. Strategies for intervention with adult children of alcoholics.

Church Advertising, Steve Dunkin. Abingdon Press, 1982. A practical guide for developing publicity materials.

The Church's Ministry with Older Adults, Blaine Taylor. Abingdon Press, 1987. Suggestions for ministry with older persons.

Experiencing Singleness: A Process of Discovery, Ed Boye (2045 Peachtree Rd., N.E., Suite 601, Atlanta, GA 30309). A curriculum for single adults.

Exploring the Road Less Traveled, Alice and Walden Howard. Touchstone Books, 1985. A guide for using the book, *The Road Less Traveled,* in groups.

Five Audiences, Warren Hartman. Abingdon Books, 1987. Suggestions for identifying adult audiences within your church.

Gifts Discovery Workshop, Herbert Mather. Leader's Guide and Participant's Guide. Discipleship Resources, 1985. Manuals for leading and participating in gifts discovery workshops.

Kids: They're Worth Every Penny, U.S. Department of Health and Human Services, Office of Child Support Enforcement (6110 Executive Boulevard, Rockville, Maryland 20852). A handbook on child support enforcement.

Launching and Sustaining Successful Singles Ministry, Dick Dunn. Singles Ministry Resources (P.O. Box 1472, Roswell, GA 30077). A workbook and cassette tape.

Make a Difference You Can See, Marilyn Magee and Evelyn Burry. Discipleship Resources, 1987. Suggestions for planning and developing ministry in your church.

Passages, Gail Sheehy. Bantam Books, 1984. Discusses the stages of adulthood.

Reach Out to Singles, Raymond K. Brown. Westminster Press, 1979. A guide for leaders in beginning and maintaining single adult ministry programs.

Singles, The New Americans, Jacqueline Simenauer and David Carroll. New American Library, 1982. Facts and information on single adult life in the United States.

Singling: A New Way to Live the Single Life, John R. Landgraf. Westminster/John Knox Press, 1990.

The Social Principles of The United Methodist Church, General Board of Church and Society. (Order from Discipleship Resources.) A discussion on The United Methodist Church's beliefs about various social issues.

The Society of St. Stephen Handbook. Discipleship Resources, 1984. A guide for providing specific and practical support to persons within your community.

U.S. Lifestyles and Mainline Churches, Tex Sample. Westminster/John Knox Press, 1990.

When Bad Things Happen to Good People, Harold Kushner. Avon Books, 1981. A discussion of God's role and place in suffering.

Who Am I Now?, Level One (ages 4-6), Level Two (ages 7-12), Level Three (ages 13-19), Robert Allers, The Beginning Experience (Central Office, Inc., 2701 W. Chicago Blvd., Detroit, MI 48206). Curriculum for support groups for children who have experienced divorce, separation, death of a parent, etc.

Sexuality Resources

Embodiment, James B. Nelson. Augsburg Press, 1979. An approach to sexuality and Christian theology.

Sexuality: Stewards of God's Gift, United Methodist Curriculum, Cokesbury Service Center. A seven-session series for adults dealing with issues of sexuality.

For More Information and Resources

For area resources (speakers, films, books, etc.), contact your public library, area colleges and universities, and community agencies.

For other audiovisual resources, write Ecufilm, an ecumenical film and audiovisual rental agency. Write for a catalog, c/o United Methodist Communications, P.O. Box 320, Nashville, TN 37202.

For other print resources, contact your nearest Cokesbury Bookstore and other local bookstores. Request a *Planbook,* a catalog of United Methodist curriculum resources, and *Forecast,* an order form and United Methodist curriculum resources guide.

Also request a free catalog of resources for church programs and discipleship growth from Discipleship Resources, P.O. Box 189, Nashville, TN 37202, 615-340-7284.

For other information about single adult ministry, contact Karen Greenwaldt, General Board of Discipleship, P.O. Box 840, Nashville, TN 37202.